## ABOUT THE AUTHOR

Raised in Maryland, MIRANDA WEISS lives in Homer, Alaska. She received her MFA from Columbia University.

# TIDE,
# FEATHER,
# SNOW

# TIDE, FEATHER, SNOW

## A Life in Alaska

## MIRANDA WEISS

HARPER PERENNIAL

NEW YORK • LONDON • TORONTO • SYDNEY • NEW DELHI • AUCKLAND

HARPER ● PERENNIAL

FIRST HARPER PERENNIAL EDITION PUBLISHED 2010.

*Designed by Eric Butler*

Library of Congress Cataloging-in-Publication Data is available upon request.

ISBN 978-0-06-171026-1

10 11 12 13 14  OV/RRD  10 9 8 7 6 5 4 3 2 1

*O madly the sea pushes upon the land,*
*With love, with love.*

—WALT WHITMAN, *Out of the Cradle Endlessly Rocking*

# Contents

# TIDE,
# FEATHER,
# SNOW

# SETTING THE NET

MEAN HIGH WATER: *n. Average height of water at high tide.*

Moving to coastal Alaska meant moving to the water life, although I hadn't known it until I arrived. Nothing is separate from the sea—not the sky, not the land, not a single day, nor my mood. I wasn't used to this. I wasn't ready for it.

IT WAS THE middle of July when John dragged out a tangle of net he'd salvaged from the beach months before. In winter, wind and surf reshuffled the beach, exposing hidden treasures—rusty bicycles, boat parts. He had wrestled the gill net from the sand and now wanted to set the net in front of the house for silver salmon that ran along the shore toward streams farther up the bay. I couldn't conceive how such a thing should be done—where to set the net, how to check it, what to expect. But John had a way of finding free stuff and asking a few questions here and there—at a potluck dinner, at the gear shop, in the neighbor's yard—and then he'd know how to do it.

John's certainty intimidated me. So I washed dishes and watched him through the kitchen window as he spread the clump of net on the lawn and got to work meticulously unwinding, untying, and straightening the whole thing out. The net took a day to untangle and decipher. When it was done, the mesh stretched sixty feet across the grass and lay ten feet deep. The float line, a line of white floats across the top of the rectangular net, would hang the net from the water's surface and the weighted lead line at the bottom would sink to keep it open when submerged. I helped John fold up the net in the way he'd learned from a friend: He took the lead line and I took the float line and we walked from one end to the other, bunching it up along the way.

At low tide the next morning, I followed John down the edge of the bluff in front of our house, lugging the hind end of the net over my shoulder. I liked to believe my lithe, curveless body, though small, was strong and capable of bearing up to whatever I wanted to do. But I slipped under the weight of the net in muddy spots the wild raspberry had left bare. The sky was a wide open blue and the white sides of gulls glinted far out on the bay. In front of us, the retreated tide exposed a mud mirror that reflected the mountains across the water. Clam holes and the coiled castings of marine worms pocked and pimpled the reflection. We weren't the only ones who had decided to try for silver salmon. Two nets were set in front of houses farther up the bay, and with the tide out, their lines and pink buoys lay idle on the flats.

John had planned it all out. We staked one end of the net close to shore, stretched the mesh perpendicularly across the mudflats, and then anchored the other end into the mud. Then we dragged the lead line away from the float line, opening the mesh. It was as flaccid as an empty sleeve and so far from the water it looked as though it would never be submerged. But John insisted that silver salmon run through the shallows. For good luck, we tied a buxom white mermaid buoy to the net. Then there was nothing left to do but wait out the tide.

EARLIER THAT MONTH, we had bought fishing licenses at the grocery store and picked up a colorful newsprint booklet that explained the fishing regulations for South-central Alaska. The sixty-page publication included colorful drawings of rockfish and salmon, maps of river mouths and bays, instructions on how to efficiently kill your catch, and detailed directions on where and how to fish. John and I had moved to Alaska not quite a year earlier and had learned that with fishing, as with everything else, there were clear distinctions between locals and outsiders: Only residents could use nets to catch fish for themselves, while tourists were limited to hook and line.

New to the town of Homer and eager to fit in and stake out our own territory, we quickly realized that Kachemak Bay, on which we now lived, was already a crowded place.

Even with its convoluted coastline and dozen islands, every bit of nature's real estate had been claimed. All five species of Pacific salmon populated the bay, fattening off its rich waters and swarming local streams. Humpbacks, orcas, and fin whales regularly plowed the water, sending the sound of their exhalations over the surface of the bay. Forests of ribbonlike kelp grew thickly from the seafloor, feeding urchin and harboring sea otters, who napped while wrapped in the green fronds. Long strands of kelp washed ashore and quickly became whips and jump ropes for children playing on the beach, or were sliced and pickled in jars. When the bay withdrew at low tide in the spring, shorebirds up from California and Mexico on their way to nesting grounds farther north crammed the flats, needling their bills into the mud for pink, thumbnail-sized macoma clams. Above, marsh hawks patrolled for the stragglers and the weak. Hundreds of snow geese owned the head of the bay each spring, and the rocky shore on the south side of the bay, which was dimpled and nicked endlessly, was as populated and compartmentalized as the oldest city block. Sea lions claimed Sixty Foot Rock as their haulout spot and occasionally lorded over the harbor, eyeing passersby with dogs. In summer, a clump of nearly naked rocks became a boisterous colony of nesting gulls, kittiwakes, puffins, murres, and cormorants. The chatter clattered loudly above the sound of the surf, and the ammonia smell of guano could burn your nose from more than a quarter mile away.

The town we had moved to called itself the "halibut

fishing capital of the world," and all summer long, charter boats ferried tourists to the mouth of the bay so they could drop lines to the bottom of the sea in search of these flat bottom fish. From time to time, a hook brought up a monstrously large halibut, which might bring its captor the annual derby loot, a prize large enough to buy a new luxury car unfit for local roads. These barn-door halibut are taller than a man, weigh more than three hundred pounds, and have to be shot dead before they are hauled onboard lest the flex of their tails swipe someone off the deck.

The commercial fishing fleet streamed out of the harbor starting in the spring. Seiners nosed into narrow fjords on the south side of the bay when salmon ran thick and followed fish up the inlet to net the oily-fleshed red salmon that pulsed by the millions into glacial rivers that emptied there. Crabbing boats docked until fall, when their harvesting frenzy would begin in the icy Bering Sea. Long-liners, gillnetters, and tenders brought fish-filled hulls back to the harbor to be unloaded by cranes. A long pipe that pumped waste from fish processing and packing plants back into the bay attracted a storm of gulls at its mouth. The commercial vessels, which docked closest to the entrance of the harbor, were being pushed aside by an expanding army of charter boats and water taxis, pleasure skiffs, and private yachts.

THE CENTER OF town squatted between the end of the highway and the beginning of the shore, and I quickly realized the sea was the backdrop for everything that happened here—a witness to weddings and deaths, to visiting dignitaries as well as to small, daily indignities. It hosted a beach barbecue for a visiting Kennedy and embraced a truck, stolen from a gay high school teacher, that had been charred and abandoned at the edge of the surf. Every house in town faced the bay or wished it did. And in places where there were no views of the sea, they had been painted on earnestly in colorful murals—inside the bank, on the side of the middle school, on a concrete wall next to the Christian bookstore, on the exterior of a shop that sold electronics for boats.

Like any seaside town, the community was continuously fortifying itself against the very thing everyone had moved here for. Years before, a sandy spit that stuck four and a half miles into the bay and marked the remains of a glacial moraine had been deemed reliable, and before long a boat harbor, hotel, souvenir shops, and fish packing plants crowded its tip. But the powerful 1964 earthquake dropped the Spit six feet into the sea, so the Army Corps of Engineers reinforced it with wood, steel, and rock. They came back again and again, each time bolstering up the sandy handle, though at high tides during storms, waves still washed over the road that ran the length of it. And to keep the sea from claiming real estate within city limits, the town built a seawall to anchor the eroding bluff. But during the first winter, waves harassed the seawall so fiercely it gave way.

The word "Alaska" was likely taken from the Alutiiq word *Alaxsxaq,* which refers to the thing the sea throws itself against. And, more than any other state, Alaska is defined by water. In Southeast Alaska, days and days of rain souse temperate rainforest, where spruce can grow to two hundred feet tall and as wide as cars at their bases. South-central Alaska, which was carved and recarved by icy glacial waves, is dominated by rushing salmon streams. Each summer, fishermen spill out of RVs in chest waders and line the edges of the region's waterways like human riprap. Much of western Alaska is low-lying river delta that gets flushed by the sea. Extreme spring tides bring the Bering Sea dozens of miles inland, so you can be standing calf-deep on tundra with no land in sight 360 degrees around you and the sea creeping ominously up your boots. The topography of the Arctic is dictated by the habits of frozen water. A waterproof layer of permafrost below its surface traps rain and snowmelt so that the landscape is freckled with lakes, in some places creating terrain more aquatic than terrestrial. And each winter, ice drives wedges into the tundra that split the ground into polygons so regular it could be the surface of a soccer ball stretched flat. Even the interior of the state, hundreds of miles from the coast, is at the whims of giant rivers, namely the Yukon and Kuskokwim. Around the hem of the state, the sea has laced a coastline so frilled it would wrap nearly twice around the waist of the earth if unraveled. And the sea surrounds Alaska's thousands of islands and claims them as its own. Here, the sea and its rivers serve as highways, supermarkets, landing strips, sewers, mail routes, and navigational markers. Water includes and excludes, carves the land, and ferries it away.

As if that weren't enough, fish carry the ocean into the very middle of the state: Each year, millions of salmon swim more than a thousand miles up the Yukon, and countless more make their way up smaller rivers and streams all over the Alaskan coast. They work their way against whitewater and fling themselves up waterfalls. So singular is their purpose that they don't eat during this time and instead digest their fat reserves while alive. The fish turn rainbow colors and white fungus spreads along their skin. The males sprout grotesque humps and their jaws contort fiercely in their fight to fertilize a female's eggs, which she lays on the gravel bottom of a stream or lake. When this work is done, they slowly die. Creeks become scenes of death and decay, strewn with stinking fish carcasses. First, gulls come to peck out the eyeballs. Then bears creep in to scavenge. And everything else arrives too: flies, beetles, eagles. Years later, when those bodies have been replaced by countless others and that sea-fed flesh has long since soaked into the ground, pieces of those fish appear as chemical signatures in the leaves of Alaska's trees. Here, the sea surges far inland to feed the terrestrial world.

MINE WAS A landlocked childhood. In the Maryland suburbs where I grew up, there was no evidence of the sea anywhere. The earth was clay, not sand. Heavy, gray-trunked trees cluttered the horizon. The air smelled of wet leaves. And when the months of summer's swampy heat arrived, we craved a breeze blown off the sea. So we piled into the family station wagon and lumbered out to the beach. First past the cornfields and chicken farms, then through the sandy stands of short pines and the tiny getting-to-the-beach towns with clapboard houses and small wooden churches. We spent a week lying on towels spread over sand too hot for the bottoms of our feet and diving through dingy waves. On the other side of the break, I floated on my back with my toes to the sky and at night I would fall asleep feeling the rise and fall of the sea inside me. I took shells home to arrange along the windowsill to remind myself of where the land stops and the water begins.

Perhaps this pull to the sea is in my genes. My grandfather was a captain in Britain's Royal Navy and served during World War II. As a young officer, he kept a scrupulous journal that documented the activities of the ship and included hand-drawn diagrams of ports, riggings, and engine parts. Later in his career, he wrote a manual about piloting the waters off Ireland's rocky coast. Maybe deep in my cells lies a need to know these things: how to navigate rocky shores, how to name the parts of a ship, how to feel comfortable with the sea.

But once in Alaska, I felt adrift and confused. I was a stranger in a place where days were quartered by the tides, where the year was marked by seasons of fish. I was marooned by words I didn't know: beam, bilge, pitch, draft. People spoke about the surface of the sea with common words made foreign: lumpy, messy, calm as glass. There were so many words to learn—no fewer than three dozen to describe sea ice, including pancake, rind, fast, and brash—and countless more to describe boat types and parts. John learned new terms quickly and used them easily, confidently. For me, learning each word became a small act of appropriation, and I felt my mouth form around these foreign sounds tentatively. "Skiff," I said to myself many times before I used it aloud. These small, open boats are as ubiquitous as cars in coastal Alaska. Skiff, skiff. The sound traveled backward from the front of my mouth, between the tip of my tongue and the space behind my top front teeth to the round hill of my tongue. Then back out to my lips, where the sound of "iff" dammed up between my lower lip and front teeth.

For years, Alaska had been the territory of my dreams and aspirations. And once I arrived, I wanted nothing else than to feel at home here. But, having grown up in East Coast suburbs where dead ends were referred to as cul-de-sacs and where my main skills were playing Chopin nocturnes and getting good grades in school, nothing I had known before seemed useful here. I was surrounded by people who boasted local know-how and carried around the knowledge of fish, tides, boats, and weather as ballast. This was how people navigated this place, and how they possessed it. And from the moment I arrived, gaining this knowledge seemed the only way to feel like I belonged.

But becoming comfortable with the feel of new words in my mouth was not enough. I had to learn their meaning, and the patterns in fish and weather, the behavior of the sea, which governs life here. I learned that on sunny summer days a strong wind would pick up across the bay. This day breeze was created when warm air rose up from the land and sucked in cold air lurking above the sea to fill its place. It could lift the surface of the bay two or three feet and aggravate tiderips, but would predictably lie down in the late evening when the temperature dropped and fishing boats returned to the harbor. I learned the cycles of the tides and studied the seasons of fish—when to expect herring, halibut, hooligan, or salmon. I needed to know the difference between a seiner and a longliner, between reds, pinks, silvers, and kings. I needed to know the feel of a following sea and the risk of wind against tide.

I learned too that to live by the sea was to be pummeled by constant change. One hour, you watched waves batter the cobbles at the foot of the bluff, and then later, the tide receded, leaving the beach silent and open-palmed. And the weather was shifty and capricious. It snowed in spring, hailed in summer, froze and melted and froze again all winter, and fall could be long and dark and wet. You could watch fronts spinning off the Gulf of Alaska, pinwheeling bands of clouds over the mountains across the bay. Some days, wispy clouds raked the sky; on others, cumulus tumbled over the bluff. Rain in town turned to snow as you drove out, and fog pressed in so thick you could barely see past the hood of your car— then you'd get up to the top of the hills behind town and find the sun blaring. Because seaside folks are used to an unpredictable sky, constancy makes them nervous. People

here got antsy with day after day of sun. And they knew
to wait out squalls beneath a tree or in a coffee shop, to
wait out the wind in a cove rather than make the crossing
from the other side of the bay.

Nothing was predictable. Nothing stayed the same. On
sunny days, the water looked deep blue or as green as jade.
Under clouds, it was a skin of mercury pulled taut or gray,
windblown silk. And, as if to mimic the sea, the town itself
was constantly metamorphosing and evolving. The school
bus garage became a pizza place and liquor store; the travel
agency moved into an old restaurant, and a hair salon took
its place. The biggest bar in town closed and sat empty
and the pottery shop became a burrito joint. Remaining
patches of green were graded and built upon, giving the
town an awkward stepped arrangement: The end of the
community college's parking lot was at eye level with a
tiny church right behind it, and a vacant shop sat on the
slope below the gravel pad it should have been built upon.

Insistent on change, the sea cares nothing for history.
The black seams of coal that lined the bluff's edge contained ancient plants. But the sea made everything new
again. Coal dropped to the beach in rectangular chunks
and, after storms, people drove trucks onto the sand to
collect it to heat their houses. Waves wore down what was
left to black grains that gathered like shadows around the
bases of rocks and in pools in the sand. Near the sea, the
earth is never still. John and I would wake to find a few
more feet gone from the edge of the bluff in front of our
rental house.

Living in a state of constant change set me adrift. So I bought a piano, sold on consignment from a shop a hundred miles up the highway. I imagined the weight and bulk of it as an anchor, something to root me and tether me home. We wrapped it in blankets and drove it down the highway in a borrowed trailer under spitting snow. It took six of us to lift it into the house. But as we moved it from one rental place to the next, dragging this anchor didn't make me feel at home.

Unpredictability and change require the sea's inhabitants to adapt or die. This creates bizarre creatures suited to live near boiling undersea vents, in subzero temperatures, in super-saline waters, in places slapped remorselessly by storms, and in the sometimes dry, sometimes drowned intertidal zone. So, when the tide goes out, anemones close in on themselves and wear shards of shell and stone as armor against the deadly dry world. Eel-like gobi fish linger in the wet spots beneath stones until the sea returns. And limpets tightly clamp their conical shells against the surface of rocks to trap the moisture they need to live. The sea is guiltless, harsh, and sustaining. So you go adrift, leave yourself to the mercy of currents, wear your skeleton on the outside, anchor yourself—or crawl under a rock.

The town was filled with an odd assortment of people who had found their own ways to live. There was the long-bearded man who carved walking sticks and sold them next to the entrance to the warehouse supermarket. One day, the cabin he'd been squatting in mysteriously burned down. There was a young loner who hiked into town from his cabin ten miles back in the hills. He wore fatigues, carried an army frame pack, and always traveled with a black mutt. In the middle of winter, he walked to his neighbors' property and shot at them through the windows of their house. There was the woman who sold tie-dyes and lived in a purple bus parked next to the diner. And there was the man who dressed as a woman, showing up at the supermarket with his wife. She was short and dumpy, he was tall and dazzling—long painted nails, gold chains, a beaver fur hat, a touch of color on the lips—a bit like a dressed-up horse.

Although the sea is fiercely whimsical, it wastes nothing. Sunlight is trapped and never let go. Calcium, which comes first into the ocean from mountains, becomes shells and teeth and backbones and all of those things all over again. The sea's frugality was contagious. Retired boats were dragged ashore and made into houses, bed and breakfasts, sweet pea planters. Old cabins were picked up and moved, reroofed, added onto. Oil drums became barrel stoves and barbecues. Old fishing nets were strung between spruce posts to keep moose out of vegetable patches. And rubber boots too worn to be waterproof were cut down into slippers, easy to put on and take off for the walk between back door and outhouse.

The town's food web was as intricate and efficient as the sea's. Money shuffled around the community continuously. Benefit parties were held in the biggest bar in town or in local schools for a boat man whose house burned down, for a woman with a gut disease, for the four widows and thirteen children left fatherless after a charter plane carrying fishermen home plunged into the sea. A few coins dropped into a jar at the drugstore helped a mother of four whose husband died of a heart attack while playing soccer with his son in the high school gym. Everyone was connected through a network of buying and selling, giving and needing, through things left at and rescued from the dump, items sold and requested over the radio, gear exchanged at ski swaps, odds and ends bargained for at yard sales. It wasn't uncommon to see your old jacket or sweater on a friend who had bought it from the local consignment store and didn't know it was yours. Sometimes "benefits" that accompanied a salary meant fish, bread, a skiff ride. Every skill was taken advantage of, and people in town were sometimes surprised to find themselves suddenly in the role of debate coach, salsa dancing instructor, or board president.

It was so obvious to eat directly from the sea that the grocery stores sold little seafood. Instead, people put up cases of salmon in glass jars, packed a freezer's worth of fish, smoked long strips of red flesh to savor and give away all winter. Those with boats threw out lines for halibut, because they knew they'd tire of salmon by midwinter. Those without begged rides. Gardeners lugged mats of eelgrass from the beach to feed their soil. They composted fish heads and tails and fed the slurry to broccoli, pea plants, and greenhouse tomatoes.

The sea takes then gives back, it cuts and calms, it

slaps and laughs and whispers. It constantly leaves small tokens at your feet—a dead seal, a still and eyeless thrush, a wrack of spotless mussel shells as blue as jewels. And suddenly, at slack tide, the wind quiets and the water stops its charging. For a moment, you can believe that everything is normal, that the sea is well-behaved and you are in control.

AT HIGH TIDE six hours after setting the net, John and I pulled a pale yellow canoe stored in the sloping garage next to our rental and dragged it to the edge of the bluff, leaving a stripe of flattened grass. A breeze was kicking up whitecaps on the bay. During the hours we'd been up at the house, the entire net had been submerged and the tide had arced the float line as it pressed into the bay. From the top of the bluff, we could see the silver side of a fish blinking in the net just below the surface. I grabbed John's wiry arm and jumped up and down in my rubber boots on the grass. We cheered. The plastic mermaid, her head tethered to the net, swung her tail about wildly as if in celebration. Seeing one fish bobbing in the net made us hungry for more.

We let the canoe slide almost entirely of its own accord down the bluff, while we slipped alongside in rubber boots. The boat was not a seagoing vessel, and sitting on the gravel beach it gaped open, ungraceful and unseaworthy. But we had nothing else. So we carried it to the edge of the water, where the bay began to stroke its lemon sides, making it dance awkwardly.

I got in the bow on my knees, and John gave us a shove as he climbed into the stern. We paddled out to where the silver salmon bucked in the net, and John directed me to pull the top of the net into the boat so that I could free the fish. The boat bobbed as I leaned over the bow and reached my hands into the cold water to grab the float line. I heaved the line and the fish trapped beneath it over the gunwale. The fish hung in a mess of net in front of me. It was a handsome silver salmon, nearly as long as my arm. Its skin was fresh, metallic, and alive. The fish had spent more than a year at sea before making its run to spawn. As it had swum up the bay, it had hit the net, which was invisible in the murky shallows in front of our house. Its head had gone through the mesh but the line had cinched the fish behind its gills where the body widened. The more the fish struggled, the tighter it was bound.

Holding the net with one hand and the fish's head firmly with the other, I traced its body back through the net the way it had entered. Its scales were slick between my hands. I pulled the blue filament over the head and yanked it out from beneath its gills. The line left dark scars where it had tightened behind the fish's small dorsal fin. When it was free, I held the contorting body, about eight pounds of nearly all muscle, against the bottom of the boat. Its gills opened and closed, struggling in the air. I reached in my back pocket for a knife and pressed it through the gills and then into the head between its eyes, hoping I was reaching its brain. Though I only half-cared, a knife into the head seemed less cruel than letting the animal bleed slowly to death. Blood leaked from the gills toward the center of the boat and scales gilded my hands.

From the stern, John worked the bow of the canoe along the float line, and, bit by bit, I pulled sections of the net into the boat and plucked out other salmon. The fish lay twitching in the bottom of the boat. We ferried them back to the gravel beach in small batches. We spent the rest of the afternoon with the fish, taking them out of the net as the tide receded. John unbound an earth-colored flounder, palm-sized with skin like sandpaper, and lobbed it into the water where it smacked and then swam away. We undid jellyfish from the mesh and they dried on the mudflats, each its own gelatinous cosmos. John worked quickly, moved decisively. I was trying to figure out how to do the same.

By the end of the day, we had nineteen fish and had lugged them up the bluff with stringers through their gills. With the evening sun slanting across the yard, we lay plywood planks on the grass, and while John filleted, I cleaned the fish as he had shown me. One after another, I slit the bellies from tail to head. I pulled out sacks of roe—like red-orange pearls, deep red kidneys, other innards of white, browns, and green. I cleaned out the bloodline, scraping the coagulated blood along the fishes' spines with my fingers. Brown, spider-sized parasites congregated around the tails. John filleted the fish, unpeeling their flesh in deep orange cakes iced in silver.

Even though the bay was rich, what you ended up

combing from the sea was always a mystery, a surprise, a gift. And despite the hours of setting and picking the net, of carrying fish up the bluff, of cleaning, filleting and packing, what we pulled from the water felt free. We could scavenge a net and borrow a canoe to fill our freezer.

It was after midnight by the time we had wrapped all of the fillets in plastic and stacked them in the freezer. A rich indigo had begun to pull across the sky, east to west. John unraveled the garden hose and we rinsed off everything on the grass—knives, planks, canoe. My hands and arms throbbed from the carrying and cleaning, and my skin smelled like fish.

The next morning, we clambered down the bluff to where we had stashed the net in a wide plastic bucket. Neighbors down the beach, with whom we'd shared bonfires and beer, had asked to borrow the net. Emboldened by our success, John had offered to set it for them so they could pick it later in the afternoon. As we pulled the net from the bucket, we realized something was amiss. The float line had severed from the net. It had been cut. And the mermaid buoy was gone. We'd been vandalized, and I had that sick feeling in my stomach of having been robbed. It was a mixture of rage and embarrassment. I knew John was already calmly scheming about how to reattach the float line and get the net back into the water as questions spun through my mind. Who did it? What had we done wrong? Had we taken someone's fishing spot? Was it because we hadn't lived here for long enough? It was too purposeful to be random. Whoever had cut the line had to have been carrying a knife and had to be willing to walk away with a voluptuous mermaid under his arm.

We walked up the beach then down. Wind had picked up on the water and it nattered in our ears. We looked for signs: the mermaid buoy abandoned in front of someone's house, resentful neighbors, suspicious tracks in the sand. We found nothing. There was no way to know who did it or why.

We trudged up the bluff to call the neighbors to let them know it would be a while before we could set the net again. John went out to the garage to look for odds and ends he could use to fix the net. I sat at the kitchen table and watched the birch tree in the yard lean against the wind. I wondered whether it was wind that helped make birch such a strong wood, and wind, too, that made these trees bear canopies of such delicately sinuous branches.

Here was the push and pull of this place. At one moment it felt like your own. But then the tide flipped, the high pressure broke, night swung its curtain in front of your eyes. The tide was beginning to turn, and soon it would rush across the mud flats toward the beach, first in a thin sheet and then in small waves, each tripping over the last. Within hours, the impressions our boots had left on the sand would be covered by water; there would be no evidence we had been there at all.

# 2

# Passage

FORECASTLE, ALSO, FO'C'SLE: *n. The section of the upper deck of a ship located in the bow forward of the foremast.*

On the day of my departure for Alaska, I sat at an empty picnic table near the edge of the dock eating my last meal on terra firma: Alaskan halibut fish and chips. The ferry I was about to board was tied up in Bellingham harbor—its most southerly port of call—and it heaved a bit, making preparatory grunts and murmurings like an orchestra warming up. The late summer sun scattered sharp shadows across the grass and wind snapped the ship's flags. It was my first time traveling on my own, and, sitting at the edge of the continent, I was completely, terribly, and excitingly alone. I would be retracing the voyage of countless others who had traveled to Alaska before me: gold rushers, early pioneers, thrill-seekers, miners, surveyors, fur hunters, fishermen, law makers, sightseers, and naturalists. By sea, the trip would take one week.

After finishing my meal, I boarded the M/V *Columbia*, a stately white and navy blue–hulled ship. Like many of the passengers, I made the low-budget choice and didn't pay for a cabin. Instead, I claimed a lawn chair that folded flat as my bed in the "solarium," a deck enclosed by three walls and roof, with radiating heaters on the ceiling. I stashed my bags and set off to explore the ship. These ships had been the workhorses of Alaskan sea travel for many years, used for commuting between coastal communities and for delivery of cars to towns where they'd never been before. More recently, the ferries had become popular with tourists as a more modest alternative to cruise ship travel.

I dashed around the ship those first few minutes aboard. A forward viewing area at the bow had movie theater–style fold-down seats. A large deck opened at the stern. A dining room, cafeteria, and lounge sat amidships. Scores of cabins with small, rounded doors were scattered around the ship, and cars, trucks, and RVs were strapped down on the lower deck. It was the tail end of the tourist season and although the ferry—the largest of Alaska's fleet of eleven—had been built to carry five hundred passengers, the ship was fairly empty.

I planted myself at the bow to watch the ship untether itself from land. Deckhands detached ropes as fat around as my thigh from the dock and wound them up onboard. The anchor chain with links the size of loaves of bread was reeled into the hull. We were off. On my first trip to Alaska, I was going there to stay indefinitely.

I had wanted to move north slowly in order to watch the landscape metamorphose and to feel the true distance that separated the life I was leaving from the one I was going toward. As the ferry chugged through British Columbia's Inside Passage, the landscape regressed: Buildings were plucked off shorelines, roads erased from treed slopes, boats disappeared from the water. Green islands emerged from the sea like knees and rounded hills of spruce and hemlock became stout mountains along the shore. It looked as though a monstrous needle had been stitched through the very fabric of the land and smocked it along the coast. The ferry moved through narrow passes where seals bobbed their bulbous gray heads off the ship's gunwales, and one morning I awoke at 5 A.M. to see the fin of an orca knife the black surface of the sea. The region wasn't entirely devoid of human artifacts. Navigational markers alerted captains from atop hills, and great swaths of forests had been clear-cut, leaving them looking naked and shaved.

Somewhere in those narrow passages the ship crossed the invisible boundary between British Columbia and Alaska. Minutes of latitude ticked by. Each hour pressed new sights against my eyes: wood cabins graying near the sea's edge, grasses combed right up to the shore, a hundred kinds of green. I was enchanted.

My romance with the largest state had begun years before, in the fifth grade, with an assignment to write a report on the state of my choice. I chose Alaska because I knew it still held undeveloped territory and pictures of it evoked wondrous things I'd never seen with my own eyes: brown bears as large as station wagons, glaciers like icy interstates through mountain ranges, peaks so sharp they looked like saw blades against the sky.

I turned in a 43-page assemblage of cursive paragraphs on lined notebook paper, magic marker drawings, magazine cutouts pasted on blank pages, and photocopied geography handouts I'd carefully filled in with erasable pen. The next week, the class held a banquet in which each student brought a dish from his or her state. My best friend studied Idaho and toted in a pan of scalloped potatoes. I brought the only dish my mother and I could think of, Baked Alaska, which involved carving a cavity in a store-bought angel food cake, packing it with ice cream, slathering meringue over the entire thing, and baking it quickly at a high temperature. One thing on the outside, something very different within: Alaska was lodged permanently in my mind.

The summer I was fifteen, I went backpacking for two weeks in the Blue Ridge Mountains of western North Carolina. Tall rhododendrons reached pink blossoms skyward at the tops of twisted trunks, and creeks ran cold and clear, unlike the one that puttered warmly behind our house. At night, I lay under a clear sky and saw more stars than I'd ever imagined and spotted satellites zipping across the Milky Way. And yet I couldn't stop thinking about *Alaska*. The mountains of the East were humped with age and the forests, crisscrossed by logging roads, seemed tame.

Eager to go north, I applied for jobs in national parks in Alaska. They were all taken. So I settled on stints of trail work in the Rocky Mountains. Here the land cleaved and towered dramatically rather than shifting gently into the kind of shallow creeks and short hills I knew back home. In the Rockies I got my first real tastes of life in wild places: hiking thigh-deep in July snow on one day and soaking in natural hot springs the next; not seeing anyone else besides our small trail crew for days at a time, then suddenly coming upon a well-appointed lodge where the lonely caretaker cooked us an enormous dinner of linguini and wild mushrooms. I drank straight from cold streams and washed in whatever trickle we had camped next to. Mail and groceries came by plane to a backcountry ranger station, where we'd return once a week for gas-powered laundry and a one- or two-day respite from our fifty-pound packs. This was the largest and wildest landscape in the contiguous states, but still I hungered for more.

I know that love had something to do with my pull toward Alaska. During college, I had never managed to find one of those normal boyfriends—a history major from a Boston suburb, perhaps, or a pre-med student who liked to jog. Instead, I fell for men in the woods— men who knew how to chop wood, pack horses, and hail bush pilots by radio. I fell for men who knew how to say nothing as the full moon rose over the piñons, knew how to recognize the butterscotch scent of Ponderosa pines, and how to enjoy a life of hard work.

I graduated with a biology degree, and as soon as I found a job teaching science to fifth-graders on the

Oregon coast, I quickly packed my bags. Between the snarled pines along the shore and the waves tumbling up toward them, I met John. A teacher in this ecosystem for years, John was a lanky man with a close-cropped brown beard and head of short, nearly black hair that peaked at his forehead. He was often quiet around people our age, but teaching drew out of him a dramatic flair that mesmerized young students. From the beginning, I was impressed by his ability to name all of the creatures in nearby rocky tidepools: buffalo sculpin, sea cucumber, opalescent nudibranch. But it was because of birds that I fell in love with him. Everywhere we went, John knew all of the birds: western grebe, Townsend's solitaire, ruddy turnstone. He kept binoculars slung around his neck at all times, and with one hand steadying them as he walked, it looked as if he was holding them against his heart. On our days off, John took me to a lush oasis in the middle of the Oregon desert that was filled with birds. We paddled a borrowed canoe to an island where hermit thrush sang from the high boughs of ancient trees. Together, we sought out yellow-headed blackbirds, lazuli buntings, and American avocets, which wade on skyblue legs.

This sudden awareness of birds was a revelation to me. I had never bothered to look at birds or to learn the names of plants and animals where I had grown up. Although I was a biology major, I had spent more time designing experiments in the greenhouse and lab than in paying attention to what was happening in the woods. I knew maples and oaks and could recognize the cooing of mourning doves, but not much more. Once you know a place's natural history, I realized, instead of the landscape feeling smaller in its familiarity, it expands exponentially. John and I spotted falcons above an old landfill and bright yellow warblers in a power line right-of-way. We spied hawks in the suburbs and watched a black cyclone of tens of thousands of chimney swifts funnel into an old smokestack to nest. John was attuned to a frequency of sound I had never known before. When we rode bikes around town in the morning, he'd point out robins when he heard their call. When we watched movies together, he'd notice which bird vocalizations had been dubbed in without regard to natural history.

During those first weeks of training in Oregon, as I became an ardent student of this foreign landscape so that I could turn around and teach it, John took notes on me. He wrote that I had looked harder than the other teachers had at the chitons, barnacles, and anemones that opened like dahlias below the surface of the water. He had seen me linger at the tidepools holding decorator crabs, which attach seaweed to their backs for camouflage, and study the inside of a rock cave, where gooseneck barnacles hung in decadent clumps. These were his field notes, containing pen-and-inks of sculpin and thrush. He tore them out of his notebook and quietly slipped them to me. When I read them, I felt as closely observed as the birds John had dedicated so much of himself to; with a naturalist's keenness, he had recorded my small movements and the things I said.

When we weren't teaching school groups, John was teaching me. When we went for walks, he pointed out which skinny trees with the narrow leaves were Indian plum, one of the earliest to flower in spring. At night, we lay in my single bed in a trailer parked just out of reach of the surf, listening to the coastal downpours against the metal roof. We felt everything was conspiring in our love: the indulgently blooming azaleas, the gracefully sculpted offshore rocks, the way the sun dangled rainbows from the sky.

John had spent a few summers studying birds in Alaska, and when he told me he was ready to go back there, this time to stay, my eyes widened. "Yes," I said. His desire to go to Alaska was an urgent craving; mine had been a long, slow ache. So we decided on a town at the edge of a bay that filled with birds each spring, where John had been offered a job teaching at a small elementary school. He drove up the highway to Alaska that summer in a packed Volvo station wagon. I stayed behind to finish my job and counted on him to meet me at the ferry dock two months later.

As THE M/V *Columbia* squeezed through close passages, I could easily spot the brilliant white heads of bald eagles sitting sentry in spruce trees along the shore. Gray gull-like birds dipped into the sea off the bow. I puzzled over my bird guide, trying to identify them. Were they northern fulmars? Flesh-footed shearwaters? Mew gulls? John would have known.

For years I had wanted to go to Alaska and yet, as I stood at the deck rail, I forgot how I had made the decision to move. I felt as though I were carrying out a plan made long ago, perhaps by someone else. I realized that once the split second had passed in which I'd made the decision to go, the rest of my life had aligned politely behind it. By the time I'd boarded the ferry, I was miles beyond turning back.

Inside the ship, I studied maps on the walls, posters about Alaskan towns, pictures of Alaskan birds. I realized how little I actually knew about the state. While low clouds wrapped themselves around the ship's windows, I imagined Homer, the town where I was going to live. I pictured a place dark with spruce, a coast of black rocks beaded with white barnacles, and scattered wooden houses that were neatly trimmed. I imagined that John and I might rent a cabin somewhere in the woods. We might live without running water, as we had heard was common among people living a little ways out of town. While in Oregon, I had subscribed to one of the community's two local weekly newspapers and in the evenings, I sat at the dinner table reading the police blotter aloud:

AUGUST 9: *A city worker at 9:42 A.M. reported graffiti painted on city property.*

AUGUST 10: *A man at 7:56 P.M. reported a black bear in the backyard of his Birch Way house.*

AUGUST 12: *A woman at 10:52 P.M. reported an extremely drunk man lying in the middle of Jackson Street. Police arranged for the man to go home in a taxi.*

AUGUST 13: *A woman at 2:49 P.M. reported a missing purse.*

I assumed the matter-of-fact, Dick-and-Jane language of these compressed stories captured the town's worst ills; it seemed quaint.

When I stood at the deck rails, I remembered how I'd stood there in my mind years before. Part of the assignment for my fifth grade report required that I imagine and write about a visit to my chosen state. Worried that I might not have enough material, I started the voyage at my Maryland home at the beginning of a tedious, six-day drive across the country on major interstates I had located on my father's road atlas. On day seven, I drove my car onto a ferry in Prince Rupert, British Columbia, for the one-and-a-half-day trip to Juneau. By the next morning, I had befriended an Eskimo man and he was teaching me how to fish off the deck. I saw puffins on rocky cliffs. I ended the story of my trip on day nine, when I drove my car off the ferry at Juneau. There, my imagination faltered, so I mentioned only that I'd spend a few weeks enjoying "beautiful sights."

Just as the maps went blank north of California before Alaska's coast had been traced, my mental map petered out once I crossed the edge of the state. I'd seen pictures of its coastline, glaciers, and big mountains. But my image of this immense state was as incomplete as an unfinished dot-to-dot. I couldn't know how it fit together—how expanses of tundra gathered like fabric around the foothills of mountains, how rivers cast off old oxbows and curves, how spruce forests scattered into treelessness, how glaciers receded, leaving giant mounds of old mountain parts aflame with stands of cottonwood and birch.

"I have lived in Alaska for a couple of years," I wrote at the end of my fabricated visit. "I really like it here. Most of my friends are Eskimos and I have learned to speak Aleut. I am going to school here and I am not sure what will lie ahead of me in the secret and mystical land of Alaska." I wonder whether anyone else in my class took their report as personally.

Two days after leaving Bellingham, Washington, the ship slipped into a narrow, liquid crease between velvety green hills. We were approaching Ketchikan, the first Alaskan port, where I would get off the ferry to switch ships for my final destination of Seward, another three days away. We were at the southern tip of the Alaska Panhandle, the strip of coastland and islands that stretches five hundred miles southeast from the state's mainland. Southeast Alaska, flush with the kind of temperate rainforest I had become familiar with in Oregon, is dotted with communities accessible only by air or by sea. Low, wet clouds parted the day we arrived in Ketchikan. At the edge of the water, a clutter of tourist shops, wood houses on pilings, and defunct logging mills glistened under the sun. Thirteen feet of rain that washed in each year had scrubbed everything in this small town clean.

But Ketchikan was filthy with salmon. Pink salmon were running up the creek in the middle of town so thick the whole place reeked. At the mouth, fish stirred the surface of the water into a fierce froth. Two local men stood on the bridge which spanned the creek near its mouth as their children dropped fishing lines over the edge. The men joked about how bad the town would smell in a couple of weeks.

After checking in to a small hotel, I clambered down to the creek. Female salmon shimmied their tails over the creek bed to dig depressions called redds where they would lay eggs. Males surged upstream, vying for the chance to fertilize. Stepping from stone to stone, I saw fish in every stage of dying and decay. For miles upstream, the bodies littered eddies, rotted in rock crevices, and lay splayed and decomposing along the banks. All around me, gulls attacked the rancid flesh.

Later, I hiked up a squat mountain on the back side of town that was flush with rainforest. The spruce and hemlock trees, which I had become familiar with in Oregon, were wide and tall. Ferns leaned over the trail, and moss fleeced the trunks of trees and every surface otherwise left bare. Below me, sunlight silvered the sea between green islands. And inland, these dense woods, striped here and there by timber harvests, stretched to the horizon. For two days, enormous cruise ships, like supine skyscrapers, pulled in and out of port. They poured out passengers who swamped the local shops for a few hours and then sucked them back in and took off.

Ketchikan looked just like the town I'd imagined was my final destination, and the doubts I'd been having about my move were replaced by the near-electric feeling of possibility that was an undercurrent of my two days there. Each step I took up the fish-strewn creek was charged with the fear of bears; one might prowl in for a meal of sluggish salmon at any time. The rancid scene of life and death playing out so pungently in the middle of town was just a small part of the life that was sparking off everywhere around me. I got hints of the locals, the community of people on the other side of the fresh coats of paint that colored the buildings within a walker's radius of the cruise ship dock. I knew there were many stories the façades didn't tell. And I recognized a new potential within myself as a young woman traveling alone, new to this town, infinitely intrigued and intriguing. If these were my first few steps on Alaskan soil, what would the next hundred bring?

In Ketchikan, where industry once thrived, it now faltered. Tourism was taking over a greater share of the market, and people were figuring out new livelihoods. The town had a jumbled appearance: Charmless storefronts abutted public displays of elegant Native art. Drab houses crawled up the mountainsides near town where lush forest was pulled in like a cloak. The timber industry left acres of scars in the foothills while tourism painted a sheen of cuteness on the few blocks that made up downtown. The riches of the place lay in its wild coastline, its acres of forests, and in the opulence of salmon that thronged in from the sea.

Forty-eight hours later, I boarded the M/V *Kennicott*, the state's newest ferry. It was smaller and emptier than the *Columbia*, and I dropped my bags in an abandoned observation room on the upper deck. Having little money and eager to exercise the sense of self-reliance I associated with Alaska, I never bought a meal on either ship. I had stocked up on dried soups, instant oatmeal, and fruit before I left and used the ships' microwaves for primitive cooking tasks.

For two more days, the ship continued up the Inside Passage in still seas buttoned down with islands and hemmed by an infinitely furrowed coast. As the mountains along the shore grew sharper, I thought about how I had grown up without topography. The land I had come from had been flat and tame. Here, undeveloped land stretched from the edge of the water as far as I could see. Whole mountain ranges were left to their own devices. Entire watersheds flowed unbothered from their headwaters to the sea. Great plains of ice were free to grind mountainsides into dust and shoot out chalky rivers.

As I leaned against the gunwale, it occurred to me how much I couldn't see, and how hard it was to grasp what I could see. A few years later, I read the account of a similar voyage to Alaska by John Muir, the naturalist and conservationist. In 1879, twelve years after the

United States purchased Alaska from an indebted and overextended Russia, Muir took a mail steamer northward from Portland, Oregon. After a childhood in Scotland and then Wisconsin, he had explored the country at a naturalist's pace. He walked a thousand miles from Indiana to Florida, and traversed much of California on foot. He fell in love with the Sierra Nevada Mountains and became an ardent voice for conservation in the West. At age forty-one, he traveled to Alaska for the first time and stood on the deck of the ship gawking at what he saw around him. He called the landscape off the bow "hopelessly beyond description," which was, for a man who spent his time scrupulously observing and documenting the natural world, no insignificant admission. I imagine what he meant was that the very scale of Alaska's coastline was dizzying, and to comprehend it all would take more than a lifetime.

Two days from Ketchikan, the ship turned west and left protected waters. As we crossed the Gulf of Alaska's stormy threshold, twenty-five-foot seas thrust the bow skyward and drove seasick passengers to seek open air in which to vomit. Having swallowed the appropriate orange pills, I stood valiantly at the bow, feeling it thump in each swirling trough, until the captain called us all back inside. Rough seas came with winds that blew so hard a cargo door was torn off its hinges. The state's brand-new boat was forced to backtrack to its last port, and the purser announced a seventeen-hour delay and free cafeteria meals for all.

In this close world, I made friends easily. A short, muscular blond guy about my age who had claimed a reclining deck chair near mine confided in me that his handgun was stashed in his truck (which was belowdecks) and that he would never be so stupid as to travel without one. I met a high school teacher from Los Angeles who had decided one day to escape his life and head north. Another man had left behind a girlfriend and young baby in hopes of finding work. He said that he would send for them. I met a nurse moving alone to a remote Native village, and a man from Long Island who had just been hired to be the director of a prestigious science center in Alaska. His girlfriend had come along for the trip, but wasn't going to stay. I couldn't help wondering whether one of them would change their mind.

We traded cameras and took pictures of each other at the bow with the coastline spread grandly behind us. We gathered at the gunwales when someone spotted a pair of whales. We swapped magazines and books. We were all in suspension—awaiting a new job, a remade life, an adventure, newfound solitude. There was no other choice but to take people as they were, which meant without an identity tied to job or geography, and with little baggage. We were in it together, bearing the two-story-high swells, the smell of vomit, the limitations of comfort. We became tribes, banding and disbanding easily—over dinner or a Scrabble board, at the deck rails, with a pack of cards. We were in the midst of in-betweenness, neither in our old life nor in the new, standing on our own clean slates. Off the stern, the sea flattened the ship's wake and erased our tracks.

Soon after the cargo door was repaired and we were again on our way, the ship slipped into Prince William Sound between glassy waters and a low ceiling of clouds. I parked myself at the deck rails and watched black and white Dall's porpoises play in the bow's wake. They dashed in and out of the emerald water that raced against the hull. Dark mountains rose like sleeping giants at the water's edge and two long islands—Hinchinbrook and Montague—closed behind us. In front of us, the sea was pulled taut. Wooded islands foregrounded the mainland darkly. Waterfalls flung thick, white cords down black slopes, and everywhere the undulations of the coastline produced an endless string of bays, inlets, and coves.

Ten years had passed since the 1989 *Exxon Valdez* oil spill, which had leaked at least eleven million gallons of crude oil into the Sound. Tides had washed the crude out of the protected Sound and swept it westward, greasing 1,300 miles of coastline—enough to blacken the beaches from Boston to Cape Hatteras. I was fourteen years old at the time, and the news stories of the spill had left indelible images in my head of birds blackened with oil, workers in rubber suits and masks trying to rinse beaches with heavy hoses, and one dead sea otter after another. But now, viewed from the ferry, the region looked pristine. I didn't know that you could dig into nearby beaches and still find oil blackening the sand. Nor that the spill had spelled both bust and boom for many Alaskans.

We stopped at Cordova, a fishing town of about 2,500 people, squeezed between mountains and the Sound. Low wet clouds had settled comfortably in town, and from the bow I couldn't see past the docks where locals lingered in rubber boots. After a few passengers and a truck or two left the ship, we were off once again.

Eleven hours later, the ship muscled into a narrow bay under a fat moon that spilled a path across the black sea like a film of milk. At the head of the bay sat the town of Seward, a community of about four thousand people who lived mainly off of fish and tourists. In the moonlight, I could see buildings cluttering a narrow shelf of land between steep slopes and the sea. My eyes scanned down a series of pools of yellow light beneath streetlights at the edge of the dock. There was John, standing in rubber boots waving up to me with both arms. He looked like he'd been here for years.

I smiled back and waved. "Awww," said the nurse who stood next to me at the rail. There was the man who was the convergence of the life I had left behind and the new one I would create. I felt a split second of disappointment. The end of anticipation is always a letdown; the beginning is already over. Those floating moments on the ferry were done, but I knew John would have another adventure planned, and then another. I threw my backpack on my back, picked up a bag with each hand, and walked through the gate.

# 3

# LANDING

SHOAL: *n. An offshore hazard to navigation on which there is a depth of 16 fathoms or less, composed of unconsolidated material.*

I arrived in Alaska just after the sandhill cranes left. These tall, dun-colored birds with red crowns fly north from California every spring to nest on grassy fields and tundra all over the state. Everyone knew as soon as they were gone. I didn't yet know that they took summer with them and left a particular silence that I wouldn't recognize for another year.

Homer, the fishing town and vacation spot where we'd moved, is in Southcentral Alaska, on the coast of the forty-mile-long Kachemak Bay. Across the bay, the Kenai Mountains rose four thousand feet out of the sea. I arrived in October. The peaks had just gotten a new sifting of snow.

During those first days, as I hadn't yet found work, when John left in the morning for his job teaching at the small elementary school, I put on rubber boots and climbed down the edge of the bluff with the help of a rope that the owners of the house we'd rented had tied to a tree and thrown over the slope. I walked up the beach to where the scattering of houses at the top of the bluff thinned to none and there was no one around.

Alone in new terrain, I did little else than explore the beach. The name Kachemak likely meant "high-water cliff" in one of the region's Native languages, and the bluffs themselves were the layered remnants of rivers. I examined seeps that leaked out of the bottom of the bluff and layers of coal that angled across the bluff's sandstone face. It was believed that the seams of coal occasionally caught fire, perhaps by spontaneous combustion. The smoldering coal would bake the shale around it. At the bottom of the bluff, I stopped at a spot where gray stones held fossilized impressions of vanished plants. If I looked closely, I could find images of leaves and branches on some of their surfaces.

Every morning, the beach donned a new garb. Twice daily, low tides pulled the bay out of its basin. The silty water withdrew from shore and left a half mile of mud-flats exposed in front of the house. On a flood tide, the water spilled across the flats quickly, until it lapped nearly at the foot of the bluff. Some days, the tidal wrack was a skein of eelgrass; on others it was a braid of yellowed reeds and empty mussel shells. Sometimes spruce chips spilled from barges loading up for Japan, and this flotsam edged the shore. At high tides sea otters floated close to shore, and when the bay flushed out, harbor seals hauled out on a glacial erratic dropped long ago by melting ice. At the month's highest tides, the bay gnawed the bluff and carried chunks of it away.

The tides brought a new timepiece into our lives. Governed mainly by the gravitational tug of the moon on the Earth's seas, the tides lagged behind about an hour each day because the moon lagged too as it circled the Earth over the course of about a month. And so much else was new: moose tracks on the sand at the top of the beach, the varied shapes of tankers that pressed into the bay, an undeveloped shore. I had expected country that was dark with trees, where the canopies knitted together over the roads. But Homer sat on a relatively flat grassy belt of land with only scattered stands of spruce. The highway came down from the north and dead-ended in Homer, which spread between two long bluffs along Kachemak Bay's north shore. The bench, as people called this meadowed swath, was like a landing between two sets of stairs: One set of bluffs led down to the beach, and the other stepped up into the hills behind town.

From any location in town, the compass directions are simple. North points toward the only way to get anyplace else: along the highway to Anchorage. To the south are the bay and the mountains across it. East means the rising sun and East End Road, which runs along the edge of the bay nearly to its head. And to the west spreads Cook Inlet, named after Captain James Cook, the British navigator who sent his ships up this long inlet in search of the fabled Northwest Passage.

Around us, the state sketched roughly the shape of an elephant's head. The Alaska Peninsula extends to the west like a long ivory tusk reaching toward Russia. The panhandle of Southeast Alaska traces the elephant's neck. The vast Interior is the animal's broad face, and South-central Alaska is dominated by Cook Inlet, the elephant's maw, which takes a two-hundred-mile-deep bite into the coast. At the back of the mouth sits Anchorage, Alaska's largest city and home to nearly half the state's population. East of the Inlet, Homer sits at the tip of the animal's lower lip, and the Spit sticks out into the bay like a long, errant whisker.

We were at latitude 59, a line that, going east, traverses Canada farther north than any of the well-known cities; cuts through Hudson Bay; nips the southern tip of Greenland; flies over mainland Scotland's head; jogs among Oslo, Stockholm, and St. Petersburg; and bisects Siberia into two long, narrow strips. We were 450 miles south of the Arctic Circle, the latitude at which the sun doesn't set on summer solstice and doesn't rise on winter solstice.

From our kitchen table, we looked out wide windows across the bay. I wasn't used to having a mountain view while I did dishes, and I wasn't used to being surrounded by wilderness. At night, a few lights blinked from the other side of the bay. Behind town, uninterrupted hills stretched to the horizon. In front of us, the bay opened to the Inlet and the Inlet opened to the wide open sea.

The town had a year-round population of about five

thousand that doubled in the summer. People were employed in fishing and tourism jobs, but the bulk of year-round work was supplied by a hospital, a mental health center, and the public school system. It was just a matter of days before I got a job teaching at a small private school where the students' ages ranged from six to sixteen. The town's mix of politically conservative Christians, hippies, ex-hippies, dislocated intellectuals, and the down-and-out created a demand for a number of small, low-budget private schools. When I arrived, in October, the school year was already a month under way, and I was hired on the spot. Over the coming months, I'd see how children around town grew up with or without running water, spending summers in town or out at remote fish camps, with parents who worked nine-to-fives or cobbled together whatever they could. It was no big deal to have an outhouse or take showers at the Laundromat.

The school where I taught was in town, not far from the beach. Up the road, the community's two main drags had a few banks, a post office, a living room–sized library, two hardware stores, a dozen churches (including Baptist, Lutheran, Methodist, Catholic, Jehovah's Witness, and Salvation Army), a few coffee joints and twice as many bars, and a handful of other shops selling new and used trinkets and necessities. I taught whatever subjects were needed for whatever students showed up: Science to sixth graders; math to tenth graders; music to all ages. During recess, I walked the students down to the beach, where they huddled in clumps behind a plywood windbreak, played kickball on a patch of grass, or threw stones into the waves.

JOHN AND I were two of the many people who ranged into town and lingered to make a first pass at enduring the long winter. No one thought we'd stay; our landlord demanded ten months' rent up front. But people took us in nonetheless. We were invited to countless potluck dinners and to birthday parties of strangers. We befriended the lesbian couple who lived just down the beach. Their ten-year-old daughter, a girl with olive skin and alarmingly green eyes, would wander over for visits unannounced. She had grown up playing on the beach, and a massive fort of driftwood—in a continuous state of being dismantled and rebuilt—stood in front of their house. Like many local houses, theirs was surrounded by a clutter of outbuildings: an old homesteader's cabin with walls papered with magazines from the 1950s; sheds slanting toward the ground; a large workshop which held lumber, empty canning jars, and out-of-season tires; and a lean-to for firewood. They often had a horse clipping the grass behind their place. He kept the scrabble of wild-growing raspberries at bay.

One evening, Kat, the mother of one of John's students, took us out in her skiff. It was my first time on the bay, and it had been years since I'd been in a powerboat. As I leaned awkwardly against the gunwale, Kat stood solidly at the tiller with her long blond hair flowing behind her. We flew over the water toward a cluster of islands off the south shore as the evening sun slanted across the bay. We slowed at the edge of a small island topped with spruce. "Radiolarian chert!" Kat shouted over the sound of the outboard as she pointed to cliffs where red rock layers somersaulted over each other. Beneath us, the Earth's crust dove, bent, and pushed its way back up. This twisted rock was the seafloor rising again. When Kat spotted a cloudy puff above the surface of the bay off in the distance, she opened up the throttle and we sped toward it. She cut the engine as two humpback whales surfaced next to the boat. They were so close we could hear the sounds of their damp exhalations, and I could imagine the wet rubber feel of their skin.

SMALL-TOWN LIFE STARTLED me. I had never known a life where you ran into acquaintances in line at the post office or while buying groceries. I had to keep my mind from drifting off because invariably I'd need to remember someone's name and make small talk. I wasn't used to buying coffee from friends or getting my car fixed by a neighbor.

The radio was the center of communication in town. The public station brought in news from the outside world in those soothing voices from four time zones away that many of us had come to know long before we came to Alaska. The radio announced important news around town too: lost dogs, missing cats, horses loose on the road. It announced events: bluegrass concerts, public meetings, and funerals. Rides were offered and requested to and from Anchorage, a 220-mile drive north up the highway ("will share the usuals"). And the radio was the way that people who lived in the Bush—off the road system, in remote places without telephone lines—sent and received messages. These bushlines were broadcast twice daily: "For Donny in Blue Fox Bay, Happy Birthday! We can't wait to see you in June. Love from Rachel and Tim." "For the Jenkins in Spruce Cove, your order's in at the Wagon Wheel Nursery. Ready for pickup."

John approached our new terrain as a naturalist. Gaining an understanding of this landscape seemed the best way to settle into it, so I followed suit. And as fall progressed, I began to see how much I'd have to learn. The names of things were critical: birds, mountain peaks, valleys, and streams. The timing of seasonal events was important too. To feel at home, I would have to sense the arrival and departure of cranes, the blooming of native plants, the fluctuations in fish. I began to learn how to look at the place. For identifying unknown birds, size and even particular coloration didn't matter much, as both could fool you over distance. Instead, I had to pay attention to where I saw them and what they were doing. To understand the geography, I needed to see how the drainages of creeks bled into rivers and where the rivers spilled into the sea. For the coast, I looked less at the waves and observed more closely what the tide was doing. I needed to be able to identify, remember, and predict.

Yet the landscape itself was relatively simple. The number of native species in a place declines as you head toward the poles because the seasons for growth and reproduction shorten. There were only four kinds of trees: spruce, alder, cottonwood, and birch. Only a few species of birds stuck around through fall and winter, including magpies, chickadees, rock sandpipers, and eagles. And you could count the number of common mammals on one hand.

But there was still so much to see. During walks on the beach, I trained binoculars on rafts of ducks on the bay and tried to see if I could distinguish, at a distance, between ravens and crows. I admired the palette on the beach—the red-orange clay, the blue-black coal, the milk white quartz veins in gray stones, the cobalt of a castaway feather from a Steller's jay, and the pine green of algae that washed ashore. With the deciduous trees undressed by fall, I could observe the particular *treeness* of the trees. The birches, now bare, revealed their wiry branches. Cottonwoods had rough, corky bark, and their uncloaked boughs terminated at tiny stumps. Spruce were steadfast, unchanged by the seasons except to offer pale new shoots at the ends of their limbs in the spring. Now leafless, alders reached out of the ground like grasping arms.

A walk around the boat harbor was an education in itself. White anemones blossomed on the undersides of floats. The pilings provided a lesson in striation: Kelp, mussels, barnacles, then thin green algae grew from below the waterline to where the wooden posts were simply damp. The seesawing ramp from the parking lot down to the harbor floats taught me about the tide: During extreme tides each month—at the new and full moons—the ramp would alternate over the course of the day between being very steep and nearly flat. I studied the docked boats. Like a naturalist, I wanted to know the right name for each kind of boat and how to identify them all. Knowing these things felt necessary to belonging here and also to surviving. I had heard stories: This was a place where a novice's mistake could kill you.

The fall's first snows on the peaks across the bay brought out the cracks and wrinkles in the rock. Rain at the lower elevations toppled the grasses and wildflower stalks left standing at the end of summer. Sunlight lengthened until its angles were sly, and each day had five minutes less light than the last. At this latitude, there were still six hours of light to lose over the next three months as the northern hemisphere leaned away from the sun. The radio announced sunrise and sunset, the minutes and seconds of light lost from the day before, and the time of the next high tide. This is how we began to keep track of our lives.

As THE DARK sky cinched down around town that first winter, my new world shrank. It was dark when I left the house in the morning to teach and dark when I returned. By dinnertime, the view from our place vanished and the windows turned to mirrors, reminding me that I had moved here knowing only John and that it would be a long, dark winter. The house clamped around us against the cold and we turned on all of the lamps. They feebly threw small patches of light out the windows and into the dark yard.

But after the first snowfall, light rose up from the ground. And snow made the endless roll of hills newly navigable. We put studded tires on the car and headed to the hills with skis in the back. Sometimes we skied to a vacant homestead cabin—a new green metal roof had been nailed on, but nothing else was square. Inside, the log walls—once chinked, no doubt, with moss—had been more recently filled with yellow spray-foam insulation. A barrel stove stood firmly on the floor and a pair of wooden skis had been tacked to the wall. The cabin hadn't been heated for years and it smelled dank. We had heard about a couple who had lived there long before. They had fished and saved money while squatting in the cabin, and now had enough cash to spend the cold part of the year someplace warm.

John would pull out the map and locate our next adventure, and our life rode this momentum of exploration. We had an endless list of new things to do together: places to ski, parts of town to explore, aspects of winter to learn about. And during these months, the sun's cold warmth forged an intimacy between John and me based on new things we shared: a flask passed between us during a ski, a thermos of hot soup sipped while sitting in the snow, our mutual distaste for the smell of exhaust that lingered long after passing snowmachines were out of earshot. We did everything together and were perfect companions— enjoying the same kind of snacks on long skis, moved by the same scenes of beauty, eager for a long day out in the cold and equally content to return to our warm, pillowed house at the end of it. These adventures weren't athletic or overly rigorous; the point was to really see the world in which we lived. It was this insistence in John that made me love him.

But he was more confident in this new terrain than I. He could talk to the neighbor about his broken snow-machine engine just as easily as to a local scientist about native birds. I was tongue-tied. And so I remained on edge, quiet and uncertain, while I began to recognize John in this life. I saw his capability around boats in a way I'd never known before. He knew how to tie them up, how to push us off, and what to do with ropes. He quickly memorized the names of all the peaks and coves across the bay while I couldn't keep them straight.

Next to John, and surrounded by dozens of capable acquaintances, I began to feel alone in my incompetence. I was in need of a friend, the kind I could laugh with uncontrollably and feel at ease with despite my inabili-ties. The women here seemed practical, no fuss. I intro-duced myself to a woman about my age who had recently moved to town. She was a Republican and a churchgoer,

I learned, two qualities that might make us incompatible. But I invited her to join John and me for an afternoon ski, and we drove up to our favorite spot and parked at the edge of the road. From there, you could look to the horizon and see endless valleys and hills: black, spruce-filled creases in an otherwise white expanse. I had learned to ski as a kid; John had learned when he was a bit older. We both loved stepping our skis through deep powder and navigating quietly around animal tracks, fortresses of alder, and the places where the snow broke through over thickets of willow. But my new friend got her skis tangled in the alders and didn't seem to like our idea of fun. So we packed up and drove back to town, and I didn't see her again. Soon after, I heard she had moved away. Half of me scoffed: I guess she wasn't up to this life. The other half wanted to run away, too.

As the snow piled up, we needed to figure out a way to keep our road and driveway plowed. Our neighbors, who lived in the only other house on the road, owned a plow truck, and we agreed to keep the road plowed in exchange for borrowing the truck to clear our driveway. Like us, the neighbors rented their place: a long, double-wide trailer fitted out with deck and shed. They had two young girls with white-blonde hair who dressed decidedly un-Alaskan in dresses and sandals. One of the daughters was named after a pop music star. They were from someplace else, and the girls' father worked up north for the oil and gas companies: two weeks on, two weeks off. Their mother, a petite woman who wore slim jeans and bleached her hair blonde, stayed home. Often, when John and I came home from work, we found that she had already cleared the snow. She was tough; she could handle a disagreeable truck, a heavy plow blade, and a snow-covered road that dropped off on either side into a ditch. I was determined to master the plow truck until I got it stuck on the side of the driveway, and John suggested it would be okay if I gave up.

Each step toward becoming familiar with the life here shunted me another one back. While walking my students to the beach during recess, a man leaned out of the window of his rusty black truck and shouted at me: "You're one of them outsiders, come up here and think you own it." I was stunned. It was impossible to know exactly what he meant. Was it because I was a teacher in a place I knew so little about? Or because my students misbehaved along the road, roughhousing in the middle of the pavement, picking up trash and then chucking it into the grass? And once, when I asked a fisherman a simple question about his work, he responded, "You must not be from around here." It was true, of course, but because I so wanted to belong, my face burned.

In this small coastal town, where tourists and seasonals flushed in and out with the weather, the length of time you'd spent in the community held more sway than what degree you had, how you made your money, or the size of your bank account or house. And everyone had been here longer than someone else. On Monday nights, I left the radio tuned to the city council meetings. Whether the discussions were about gravel mining, timber sales, or what the town should do with a small windfall of cash, citizens always prefaced their comments by saying how many years they'd lived in town.

But their short histories were nothing in comparison to the stories told by petroglyphs of people and marine mammals on rock outcroppings along the bay's shore. The Kachemak Bay region had been inhabited for thousands of years. A handful of Native cultures (including Sugpiaq Alutiiq and Dena'ina Athabascan) made their home here—arriving by sea and by land to take advantage of the rich ocean resources and protected water. But by the time the Russians ventured into the bay in the late 1700s, hungry for new riches, few Native settlements remained. In a small Native village on the bay's south shore, the Russians set up a trading post to ship pelts back to Russia. They distributed influenza and put up a church.

Across the bay from where the Russians set up shop, Homer began as a coal outpost. By the turn of the nineteenth century, American coal men mined the seams in the bluffs along the beach and laid a railroad from there to the tip of the Spit, where a deepwater anchorage allowed ships to dock at any tide. Gold seekers also landed among the clutter of buildings the coal miners had raised along the bay. Locals named the town after a swindler, Homer Pennock, who had lured a crew of optimistic lads north from as far away as Denver in search of gold. Although he assured the men otherwise, Pennock had never been to Alaska before. When they failed to find riches, most of the men took off farther north in search of gold, but Pennock returned to California.

Coal mining proceeded in fits and starts. The coal here was of a low quality and had a tendency to self-ignite, and it was expensive to ship to market. So, as with many frontier towns, the local economy changed numerous times after the arrival of the white man. Some Homer men turned to breeding wild foxes for fur, rearing them on the bay's islands where they could be let loose to den and breed on their own.

Early settlers here found it easier to dock boats on the south shore of the bay than on our side. Short piers were built off the steep rocky beaches across the bay, providing an adequate draft of water regardless of the tide. In front of the house where John and I lived, and elsewhere along the north shore, mud flats extended far out into the bay, so landing here had to be scheduled for high tide. Once the water retreated, a vessel would be stranded on the flats until the sea returned twelve hours later. Industry sprang up, then, more readily on the south shore. Canneries were built to process salmon that ran up creeks and rivers across the bay, and herring salteries preserved and packed these oily fish, which spawned on the south shore. For years, Homer remained a desolate outpost served by larger communities across Kachemak Bay.

By 1915, new settlers from the states found that the land around Homer was ideal for homesteading. Native grasses grew thickly and could be scythed and fed to cattle in winter. The maritime climate was mild with adequate but not too much rainfall. Extensive stands of spruce provided timber for homebuilding, and good water seeped in springs and ran plentifully in streams. These new settlers kept cattle and horses and grew cool-weather crops—cabbage, potatoes, sturdy greens. At the head of the bay, wide grassy river flats provided excellent pasture. But living off the land wasn't easy. The soil stayed cool well into spring, and rain often disrupted haying and harvesting seasons. The winter cycles of freeze and thaw wreaked havoc on plants. Few local markets existed for farm goods, and farmers were dependent on shipping companies based in Seattle or farther away to bring supplies and transport goods for sale. It was clear from the beginning: If you didn't know the place well, know it intimately, you would starve or have to go somewhere else. This is what was important: frost dates, signs in the weather, where to find wild food, when and where the fish ran, how to stock up for the winter, what the tide was doing at all times, how to read the surface of the sea.

At the corner of one of the main intersections in town, an old log cabin sat empty on an unkempt lot. It was a relic from the homesteading days. The original owners had built it on an island off the south shore of the bay where they lived for a time. Then they took it apart, barged it to the north shore, put it back together again, and set up a small mercantile in a tiny, attached shed. Theirs was one of the first stores to sell goods in Homer that, until then, could only be purchased across the bay. Other remains of history were scattered around town too. You could drive by an old stick-framed Civil Aeronautics Administration building, constructed in the 1940s with an influx of wartime federal funds. Built for providing weather briefings and other information to pilots, it now stood, mostly forgotten, in a junkyard a few miles out of town. And homestead cabins scattered around town were in different degrees of abandonment and repossession; some were falling apart, while others had been dressed back up and were again in use. People remembered when you could dial just four digits to make a local call. These days, we had to dial the exchange, but since it was the same for everyone in town, we remembered each other's phone numbers by only the last four digits.

John and I quickly befriended a family that had a modern sort of homestead fifteen miles out of town and six miles off of pavement. Taro and Cynthia lived in a yurt, a circular house with a diameter of twenty feet that they had bought as a kit and raised with the help of a few friends. They had no nearby neighbors. Their daughter Kaya, six, was one of John's students, and their son Ghen, four, would be in a few years. Taro, a short, sturdy man whom people sometimes mistook for an Alaska Native, was from Japan. He fished during the summer and worked construction during the rest of the year. Cynthia, from upstate New York, did various jobs and took care of the kids. John and I admired their scrupulous resourcefulness: They filled their chest freezer with fish every summer, grew a garden, constructed their own outbuildings, and made do with no running water and very little space. And we admired their art. Cynthia made clay pots and dreamed of the day when they would build a studio for her and her husband to work in. Taro was a carver and built toys for the kids out of wood salvaged from construction sites and the beach. John and I often went to their place to ski or to share dinners of salmon and large bottles of red wine. Cynthia took us down to the spring where they filled water jugs. She showed us the bathtub Taro had carved out of a solid trunk of driftwood cedar. I was in awe of their handmade life.

On New Year's Eve, John and I drove out to their place on a road white with new snow. It was the coldest night since we'd arrived in Alaska, well below zero. From the road, we skied down to their house under a sky cleanly pricked by stars. They had set lighted candles in small pockets dug into the snow, illuminating the way to the yurt. Inside, a dozen or so people sat on whatever they could find, drinking rhubarb wine and beer, sharing food. Most of the guests were neighbors who had skied over or traveled by snowmachine. Taro cut thick strips of raw flesh from a three-foot-long king salmon he had caught and frozen whole the previous summer. Cynthia spooned hot rice with fish and seaweed into bowls for the kids, while we ate sashimi. Wine and heat from the wood stove flushed our faces pink. A bonfire had been going in the snow-covered yard all day, long enough to melt a wide pit. When the yurt got too crowded, we went outside and stood around the fire with bottles of beer freezing in our hands.

The circular house sat on a snow-covered field that sloped down into a creek drainage. The place was surrounded by untrammeled, unbroken snow. Cynthia and the kids had built a wall of snow next to their house and illuminated it with candles. And they had pushed their boots through the snow in the yard, drawing swirling patterns in its surface. For these artists, snow was a canvas, the night sky a backdrop, and light was paint. At midnight, Taro struck a metal oil drum he'd hung from spruce posts as a gong, and the sound pulsed through the dry air into the valley below us. This, I thought, was an exquisitely beautiful life.

New Year's ushered in the bulk of winter. The lip of the bay iced and cracked. Hoarfrost crept down the beach. Plows drove through town, pushing snow into chest-high ridges in the middle of the road. Later, after the roads had been cleared enough that cars could pass, a huge truck came to vacuum up the snow. A vacant lot on the edge of town became a mountain of dirty, discarded snow that would last long into spring. On cold mornings, with temperatures in the teens or below, John would go out in the dark to the sloping garage next to the house and plug in the car's engine block heater. After tea and breakfast, the car would be warmed up enough so that it didn't cough so darkly when it started.

It snowed for months, and the flakes endlessly erased

themselves on the liquid surface of the bay. In February, avalanches up the highway closed the road to Anchorage for a week. This was the only road to anywhere, and cargo came into town by truck. Milk disappeared from grocery stores, then bread. Finally, a plane came to restock the store shelves. For days, people were stranded in town, in Anchorage, and at all points in between.

As the months went by, I learned signs. A snow sky was obvious: It was heavy and silent, a down comforter quietly shaking out its feathers. Dry days were colder, I learned. And on the coldest days, snow didn't even bother to fall. I learned that Jupiter and Saturn traveled across the night sky paired. I could train a scope on Jupiter, the brighter point, and see four of its moons. I thought about Galileo, who had watched them four hundred years before. Windy days, I found, were the crows' favorites. This was when they played. They hovered and danced, collected and dispersed. I learned how winter was measured: by whether the floatplane lake in town froze solid enough for stock car racing; by how many days of good, clean ice there were on the lake behind the airport for skating; by how often the power went out and for how long; by the number of feet of snow that accumulated in the hills.

In late winter, as patches of tired grass began to show through the snow, moose roved into our yard. A yearling decided he liked a spot next to the house where two exterior walls sheltered a triangle of grass. After spending the night there, the animal left behind a scattering of long white guard hairs on the flattened grass. Owls visited the

yard too. A great gray owl perched at the top of a cottonwood, and magpies flew in to harass it. We watched
the neighbors' cat steal up a birch tree toward a perched
bald eagle. As the cat got closer, the bird eyed it indiffer-
ently. The standoff ended when the eagle upped and flew
away. Coyotes slinked across the mudflats in front of the
house, and a decadently plumed male pheasant strutted
across the yard to impress potential mates.

In the spring, winter's carbonated sky went flat as the
darkness leaked out of the night, making stars lose their
luster. The sun crept out of the southern sky, arcing widely
toward the north. We had been gaining five minutes of light
each day and by late May, there were sixteen hours of daylight. There was a mania to this time; the days were getting
so long that it seemed we had two days inside each one.
After John and I came home from work, the sun shone for
hours and we wanted only to be outdoors. Nights never
fully darkened and sleeping felt irrelevant. That spring, as
red tulips we hadn't planted petticoated the house, ferns
pushed their curled fiddleheads through last year's dead
growth. We picked them and panfried them in butter.
Horsetails shot up in diminutive forests along the roadsides. Fields of chocolate lilies bloomed in cocoa-colored
flowers, which drooped earthward and smelled of rot.

By this point, I had learned that there were two ways
you could live here: the particular way of life this place
afforded or the way you could live anywhere else. Even
twenty miles out of town, some people lived with wall-to-
wall carpeting, satellite dishes, and office jobs. For John

and me, it seemed important to live in the unique way we could here. So we experimented with self-sufficiency. In the fall, we had made jars of rosehip butter, a sweet paste the color of rust, from the fruit on bushes that grew around the house. I couldn't decide if I liked it, but I ate it anyway, spread onto whole wheat toast sliced from loaves I'd baked myself. This meal was sturdy and practical; at least, I thought, the vitamin C-laden hips would ward off scurvy. In the spring, we made a dark green concoction like pesto from the young shoots of stinging nettle that multiplied in a wet spot in the yard. We canned jars of clam chowder using clams we dug from the mudflats in front of our house, and we ate whatever wild thing we could: urchin roe, mussels that washed onto the beach in clumps, fireweed shoots, wild mushrooms. We planned a garden and started seeds next to the window.

For a week in May, sandpipers arrived by the tens of thousands; the bay was their stopover point to their nesting grounds in the north. Gulls and terns took over the taiga near the airport. This hummocky area of stunted spruce provided ample nest sites. Red-necked grebes built floating nests on the floatplane lake and put up with the engine noise. The cranes returned in a dramatic *V*, and for a day or so, this was all everyone talked about. A flock of feral pigeons loitered at the harbor looking urban and out of place. Salmon threw themselves up local streams. The spectacle of summer, I realized, had begun.

At this time of year, the chorus of birds was continuous. Although robins are known as morning birds, here they sang until well after midnight, and didn't get up at dawn. John identified the melodies that began hours before we woke: the three-note calls of golden-crowned sparrows, the delicate fluting of hermit thrush, the incessant solos of kinglets. In the evenings, orange-flecked varied thrush sounded their referee whistle calls from the tops of spruce, and snipe, stocky birds with long bills, showed off in the sky: They circled and dove and let out a ghostly, ascending sound created by air rushing through their tail feathers. As John and I tended our garden starts, nothing seemed more important than growing food and learning the birds who made those calls.

# 4

# PEOPLE'S LIVES

TENDER: *n. A vessel attendant on other vessels, especially one that ferries supplies between ship and shore.*

T om Watkins's cabin sat so far over the edge of the bluff it looked like it could tumble down to the beach any day. It was a tiny structure—fifteen by fifteen at best, with a low loft up steep, ladderlike stairs. A few skinny alders seemed to be the only things that kept his bit of flat earth cut out of the edge of the bluff from sliding into the sea.

The view from Homer's bluff was so seductive it inspired impractical and idealistic construction; the bay flushed out silver, turquoise, or deep blue—depending on the weather—into the mouth of Cook Inlet, and a range of opulent peaks, specked year-round by snow, strung across the horizon on the other side of the water. This vista lured people into building where they shouldn't—in places where the bluff lost a foot of land per year as its face constantly eroded. The land slid out from beneath luxurious, glass-fronted retirement homes and steadily crept away from vacation cabins built on the edge.

I met Tom on an airplane when John and I were flying back to Alaska after our first trip away since we'd moved to Homer. He was in his early or mid-sixties, I estimated, and had a long face, pale blue eyes, short gray hair and a tidily trimmed gray mustache. He was tall, big-boned, and stiff, and joked about the uncomfortable seats. By the time we touched down in Anchorage, I had promised to show him how to use email on one of the two computers recently installed in the Homer library for the public. Tom wanted to communicate with his daughter, a lawyer in Arizona, but had never used computers before. In exchange, he said, "I cut fish out on the Spit. I'll take care of you." This meant free food.

Over the next months, I visited Tom from time to time at his cabin, which was barely a quarter mile from where the highway into town narrowed into the main thoroughfare. "No need to call," he told me. "Just come by. I'm always home after dark." It was the time when summer was rapidly becoming fall. Fireweed seed pods were twisting off along the roads, sending white fluff someplace else. A steep set of wooden stairs ran down the edge of the bluff to Tom's house from the parking pad where his beige Cutlass waited until daylight. He was bowlegged and his knees were weak. He didn't take the stairs after dark, especially not these days when the nights were cool enough to drop a slippery layer of frost on every surface. A couple of guys from the fish processing plant had built a handrail out of two-by-fours along the stairs, but that wasn't going to be enough to keep him from falling.

The cabin was a mess. Old newspapers and food wrappers littered the painted plywood floor. The place smelled like the bottom of a beer can the day after you thought you'd emptied it. There was no running water, and dirty dishes piled in the dry sink. A plywood outhouse sat among alders too short of a walk from his front door. Tom hauled in jugs of water that he filled at a free tap outside the main supermarket in town. He washed his dishes in plastic tubs balanced on the rails of the deck which stretched around the cabin. He emptied them over the railing when he was through.

His place would have been called a "shack" by my friends back East. But here, no one used that word. A small house, even a dingy one, was a cabin, an A-frame if it had a steep peaked roof that sloped down nearly to the ground, or just the neutral "place." People didn't judge how other people lived.

Tom decided he didn't want to learn to use email after all. "Nothing's wrong with a phone call!" he concluded. Instead, I stopped by Tom's just to visit. I'd gingerly clear old newspapers and beer cans from the padded blue vinyl van seat he used as a sofa. The mess depressed me, but I was drawn to his stories. Tom would deliver an update on the one-armed woman he was sort of dating. She also worked at the fish processing plant, and had given him the painting of a wolf howling under a full moon that hung crookedly on his gray wall.

Tom was from Ogema, Minnesota, a tiny town in the state's poorest Indian reservation, a rectangular patch of prairie interrupted by lakes and hardwood forest in the northwest corner of the state. His father had been one-quarter Ojibwa, his mother a little more than three-eighths, which made Tom, as he described, Indian enough to get free health care at the reservation clinic. He told me about his ex-wife, a beautiful Indian woman who had left him years before, and about his son, who had been badly injured in a motorcycling accident and since then had grown too fond of beer and not enough of work. Tom went back to Minnesota each winter, where he took care of his son and visited his mother, a ninety-two-year-old woman who was deposited once a week at the local library to read aloud to children. Some people back home still lived the Indian way, Tom told me. He described the annual wild rice harvests as he sipped from a can of Pabst in a stained pink recliner. In late summer in northern Minnesota, people took canoes onto shallow lakes where the rice plants grew thickly in the water. They pulled the tops of the stalks over the boat and knocked the kernels into the bottom of the canoe.

Sometimes Tom shared meals with me—stir-fry he'd cooked with a seasoning packet from the store which turned the whole thing into a salty, brown goo. I knew I should be wary; the hygiene situation was sloppy. But I ate his cooking anyway, and didn't refuse beer when he offered, which he always did. When Tom went back to Minnesota for two months in the winter to take care of his son, I collected his mail and checked on his place. I forwarded envelopes that looked important. Tom wasn't the friend I'd been looking for, but he needed the help and appreciated the company of a young woman willing to listen.

HOMER HAD BEEN Tom's retirement plan. He had spent his working life as a machinist and he deserved a rest. Instead, he'd gotten himself hired at one of the fish processing factories where he stood at a stainless steel counter cleaning and filleting fish all summer. Sometimes he steaked them out with a band saw. He liked the work. Tom had befriended the owners and he was able to come and go about as much as he pleased.

The summer before John and I moved to town, the big commercial seafood plant—called Icicle Seafoods—had blown up, sending a cloud of ammonia up the bay. It had been a mythic event, talked about for years afterward. Luckily, no one was killed. Much of Homer's economy had revolved around Icicle. Everyone we knew had done a stint there or had a friend who had. Tom talked fondly of Billy Pendleton, the man who, with his wife, owned the seafood plant where Tom worked. It was a relatively young business that packaged mainly the fish tourists caught on charter boats; it would freeze the fish and send it back home for them. They had recently expanded their place and dressed up the outside to be cute. They were doing a tidy business, hiring dozens of fish cutters every season who wore orange bib overalls and rubber boots and cleaned, filleted, and packed fish all day at the back of the place. The more photogenic counter crew worked up front where long freezer cases offered vacuum-sealed seafood to tourists at prices no local would pay.

Tom and Billy Pendleton drank together some days, and Tom worried that Billy drank too much. This could be serious, I thought. I rarely left Tom's place without having emptied three cans of beer myself, and Tom had often been drinking when I'd arrived and was still drinking when I left. Tom admired Billy, and told me how Billy had promised to gather a crew of guys to put an addition onto Tom's cabin at the end of the season. He said that Billy would have his guys put a new roof on the place too. Tom would use the extra room as his bedroom when he was too old to climb the steep stairs up to the loft. It was insurance against Tom's old age.

When Billy died suddenly from a heart attack the summer after John and I arrived, word spread quickly around town. I knew it would hit Tom hard. For a few days, I tried calling him, but no answer. A couple weeks later, I stopped by and Tom's eyes grew wet as he talked about his friend. Who would make sure the extra room was built? I wondered. Who would take care of Tom?

"You make your own family up here," a woman who had moved from Wisconsin once told me. Helping Tom out—taking in his mail when he left town, checking up on him every so often—was a way for me to feel useful, to grow roots in a community that sometimes didn't feel like my home. I wanted to feel connected here—linked by giving and needing. And I never left Tom's place empty-handed. He often stuffed a plastic grocery bag with treats—bags of wild rice gathered by friends in Minnesota or packages of fancy frozen seafood he'd liberated from the plant because the seals had broken. Sometimes I returned home with smoked halibut, scallops, or king crab legs nearly as long as my arm. But with few skills to offer, I felt I would never be useful enough. Tom could never count on me like he had counted on Billy.

PEOPLE MOVED TO Alaska to find themselves, but also to get lost. After five years or a decade in the state—where no one bothered you about how you lived, where you could get by working long summer days and then hole up or go south all winter, where freedom from restrictive zoning laws meant you could do what you wanted with your property—how could anyone go back? A young guy I knew who had grown up in Homer but left to get a degree at a prestigious college on the East Coast told me one afternoon, "I just couldn't find a place for myself back there, so I came home." High school graduates who did leave—for college, adventure, or work—often found each other Outside, fell in love, and came back. The state is a mixture of back-to-the-landers and misfits; of people who are escaping a life elsewhere as much as they are embracing the particular one they can find here; of well-scrubbed and short-coiffed military personnel dropped in from someplace warmer, or veterans who came here decades before looking for a certain kind of peace; of suburbanites; and of Native people straddling the modern and the old. I was like many other new arrivals: a recent college graduate in search of some indefinable hybrid of adventure, wilderness, and what I imagined would be a simpler life. I think we all wanted to know what we would look like in front of a backdrop of wilderness, who we would become once the fancy clothes and high ambitions were stripped away. For many of us, Alaska seemed the only place to figure this out.

This state has long been considered a last resort. During the Depression, the Civilian Conservation Corps scattered the otherwise unemployed across even the most remote stretches of Alaska to carry out federally funded projects; they restored totem poles, raised musk ox corrals, leveled remote forests, and dug latrines. Also as part of the New Deal, in 1935 some two hundred down-and-out farm families were shipped from the northern Midwest to Southcentral Alaska and deposited on a vast stretch of spruce-littered land that was intermittently boggy and dry. This was the Matanuska Colony, and the job of the colonists was to farm, improve the land, and convince others that it could be done. They arrived in early summer, lived in wall tents that had been thrown up by itinerant workers also brought in from someplace else, and got acquainted with their new world: with the tides of mosquitoes, with the Chugach Mountains shadowing them in the mornings, and with the dampness that clung to the land even though there wasn't much rain. Little more than a decade later, two-thirds of the settlers had left.

From early on, everyone had designs on the far-off territory. During World War II, a New York congressman proposed the relocation of unemployed urbanites and Jewish refugees from Europe to Alaska. A group of Rocky Mountain businessmen formed a corporation to invest in the plan, but Alaskans were vehemently opposed. They needed more people on the frontier, they claimed, but those with "fortitude." And they had had enough of outside interests plotting their future for them. While shipping off the destitute and hundreds, if not thousands, of refugees to the North seemed an attractive plan to entrepreneurs and urban politicians who might otherwise have to deal with them, neither scheme was carried out.

Many believed that this "fortitude" was made, not born, in the territory. One hundred years ago, government men considered Alaska to be proving grounds: The fickle sea, the sharp cold, and the uncertainty of survival would rear a breed of tough men—sturdy, seaworthy—ripe for the navy. And still, today, there was a sense that if you didn't toughen up, you had to leave. "They didn't last," we would often hear about people who moved south soon after their Alaskan debut.

Sometimes I wondered about my own fortitude. Could I last in a place where winter mornings required a long ritual of waking up, layering on warm clothes, heating, clearing snow, and de-icing? Where summer morning light shot you out of bed at 5 A.M.? Could I survive in a place where few other people seemed to doubt their own ability to survive?

I was surrounded by people who came from someplace else. And everyone had a story about how they'd come, why they'd stayed. A young woman who had run the local head shop in the 1980s selling tie-dyes and pot pipes had bought half an acre with a vast ocean view, then left for sixteen years to get career, husband, and kid taken care of before she returned and built a house on the concrete foundation she'd poured more than a decade earlier. It seemed she had come home. Her hair had gone gray, her slinky figure had filled out; she had morphed from party girl to teacher–mother–wife and hoped no one recognized her from before.

Another woman told me she'd arrived by ferry with fifty dollars in her pocket. Now she owned the bakery in town. I befriended Tammy, a woman in her forties with short brown hair streaked platinum in the front. She had left southern California for Alaska more than twenty years before, when she was twenty-two, beautiful, and in love. She had raised five babies in an aluminum trailer fifteen miles out of town while the father of her children went off for weeks at a time to fish. Tammy remembered the cold, dark mornings of winter when she coaxed her older kids out the trailer door to walk alone to the main road to meet the school bus. Being a mother like that was an act of faith. She sewed clothes, baked bread, and kept the trailer warm. When she couldn't stand the isolation any longer, she left the fisherman and moved the kids to town.

In Alaska, where many people ended up scrabbling a life together that would be considered nontraditional anyplace else, the politics of libertarians and liberals sometimes overlapped. Shuffling into city council chambers to vote, ardent conservatives who wanted to be freed from government and hippies who wanted to move back to the land and be freed from modern life could find some common ground on the far side of the political curve. Alaska's first elected officials after statehood had been Democrats; they saw statehood as a way of gaining home rule and independence from outside interests. But over the decades, the politics shifted. Most of the state's elected officials could best be described as paradoxically Republican: They hailed from the political party that seeks to shrink government, but worked to build expensive infrastructure of dubious necessity and did their best to funnel federal funds into the state for outlandish capital projects, such as a $300 million bridge to a tiny island and a $700 million port expansion for no obvious purpose. Despite the state's mythic character as fostering independence and rewarding the pioneering spirit, the Last Frontier relies more on federal assistance than any other state.

Even half a century after Alaska became the forty-ninth state, thereby gaining (residents thought) significant autonomy over what happened within its bounds, some people still view Alaska as a colony controlled by corporate investors and federal managers. More than half of the state's land area is held by the federal government, and corporations from elsewhere feed off Alaska's natural resources. Outside capital is pumped in to extract wealth from the state's remote and weather-beaten landscapes: oil and gas from the shore and below the waters of the Arctic Ocean; zinc, lead, and silver from a vast hole in the ground in Northwest Alaska, where a single fifty-five-mile-long road leads to a port that is ice-free only in midsummer; gold from vast pits dug deep in the Interior; old-growth timber from inconvenient rain forests that cloak Southeast Alaska's coastal mountains.

Although many Alaskans boast of their fierce self-reliance, Alaska is in many ways a welfare state. There is no income tax here; the state did away with it during the boom following the 1968 discovery of the nation's largest oil deposit in Alaska's Arctic. The state pays each resident merely for living here. This annual check, called the Permanent Fund Dividend, the PFD, was instituted in 1976 and is a payment of earnings on oil and mineral revenues invested by the state.

Oil wealth has had the surprising effect of making Alaska more dependent on outside investors, not less. Oil and gas activities provide nearly all of the state's income; oil pays our teachers, paves our roads, and puts troopers in their shiny white SUVs on our highways. No one knows what will happen when the wells run dry. And because state income ebbs and flows with the price of oil, what happens in the Middle East can determine whether a hockey rink gets built, a library buys new books, or a cop shop gets a revamp. But no politician would dare tamper with the PFD, let alone reinstate an income tax. And hunger for the PFD checks, which arrive in post office boxes each October, ensures that every Alaskan has an interest in development of resources in the ground around us. During the weeks before the checks are sent, ads blare for big-ticket items: new cars, high-octane snowmachines, tickets to Hawaii. "Put your PFD down and pay no interest until January!" The first year I was eligible to receive the PFD, the payment was the second highest it had ever been: $1,850.28. Like many Alaskans, I used the money to buy a plane ticket to see my family back East. As much as I wanted to make my home here, the windfall helped me and many people around me practically live in two places at once.

HAVING GROWN UP just outside the Capital Beltway, I had to adjust to the way most people here weren't racing to get ahead. They were not concerned about their professional growth, about adding stripes to their resumes, or about finding challenging job opportunities. Here, people weren't defined by their jobs. The paper girl had a degree from Stanford and was bilingual. One of the local cab drivers was a lawyer. Doctoral degrees meant nothing when your car slipped off the road, when it was moose season, or when the northern lights struck us all dumb with awe.

Many people had come to the state for adventure, silence, and wide vistas. But the landscape could be as debilitating as it was liberating. As soon as I started teaching, I heard about FAS, fetal alcohol syndrome, which is caused in babies when their pregnant mothers drink. The syndrome results in an odd assemblage of characteristics, including mental retardation, short noses, small chins, and thin upper lips. I learned that Alaska had the highest FAS rate in the world. Babies born to alcoholic mothers in Bush villages had been adopted by families in town, where they grew up, went to local schools, and tried to live normal lives. But the statistics were dismal. Alcohol killed proportionally more people in Alaska than in any other state. And here, we had high drunk-driving rates, too. The radio played public service announcements that warned against huffing gasoline, paint thinner, glue, and other toxins that teens could find in nearby workshops and garages. In Alaska, suicide rates were twice the national average, highest among young Native men in rural areas, and most common in the spring. Was it enduring the long, dark winters? The unceasing wind that could find any chink? The constant blare of the summer sun? The fragile—often failed—economies? That was a level of desperation I couldn't imagine; these hardships were still novel to me.

Some people thought the melancholy was a result of a lack of things to do. In the spring, we dug out from winter. In the summer we stocked food. In the fall, we got ready for winter. And then we just waited it out.

The only thing there was more of in town than bars was churches, and we weren't sure whether these things were unrelated. Typical Friday night entertainment was local kids performing in a play or dance show, a band from up the highway playing covers of Led Zeppelin and Foreigner at a smoky bar, a Hollywood blockbuster showing at the single-screen theater three months after it was released in the rest of the country. But when something special came—a band from Outside, an unusual art exhibit, a well-known author—everyone went. It was like having a party with all of your friends that you didn't have to clean up after.

So many things that make sense elsewhere make no sense in Alaska. Except for some of its far-flung Aleutian Islands, the entire state—which, if laid across the others, would stretch from Georgia to California—encompasses only a single time zone. And in the fall, we put our clocks back with everyone else so that, as we are already losing five minutes of light each day, we are suddenly plunged into afternoon darkness. The director of the school where I taught told me it took the students months to get over the time change. At least one elected official in Alaska reported that she received more letters about daylight saving time than about any other issue. And here, it makes sense for services to come to people, rather than the other way around. Nurses, dentists, and beauticians fly into remote villages across the state. And Alaskan school districts were using the Internet to deliver classes to the child rather than the reverse.

HOMER WAS KNOWN as a place where people ended up staying after their cars broke down. The saying was: "It's all downhill to Homer," which meant that it was easier to come to town than to leave. A friend who grew up in the Midwest and was now a father of two once told me, "This place isn't so great, it just has a great view."

But people had fought for this place. Nearly three decades before, the state had sold access to patches of the seafloor in Kachemak Bay to oil and gas companies. A jack-up rig, a floating drill rig with retractable legs that stood three stories above the surface of the water, was barged in. But when the rig got stuck in the mud and began to leak oil, fishermen and other residents were furious. A pilot who lived on the undeveloped side of Cook Inlet and referred to himself as "the Bush rat," campaigned for governor on a platform of keeping oil and gas out of Homer's bay, and he won. The state bought the access back from the companies. Recently, however, oil and gas interests were creeping toward town by land, in some cases drilling in people's backyards without their consent, which they could do because the state holds title to resources beneath nearly everyone's lawns.

This was a place people had worked to protect, but also, naturally, a place people abused. Some houses were ringed by an obstacle course of junk cars, defunct fishing equipment, earth-moving machines, and building supplies. Although you could leave a car at the dump for free, dead vehicles could be seen all around town, slowly rotting.

One day a year the borough towed away abandoned cars, no questions asked. The radio announced this day in advance; all you had to do was push the car onto the edge of a public road.

In a community so dominated by its natural surroundings, it was surprising how landmarks were often more about people and less about the landscape. When giving directions, someone might say, "You know the tan house with that gigantic spider they nailed to the outside for Halloween years ago? Well turn right there, and go a quarter mile." Or, "I'm not far past the house of the guy who dragged that old castle into his front yard." Mostly, people explained where they lived by how many miles from town they were: "I'm eleven miles out East Road." Or, "You gotta go seven miles up the North Fork, then turn left after the dip."

Racial diversity was not something Homer bragged about. It was a white town, save for a few Natives, an occasional black person, the families who owned the two Chinese buffet-style restaurants in town, and a handful of Latinos, many of whom orbited around the Mexican restaurant—owners, busboys, patrons. But Homer did boast diversity of character and constitution. I had never seen so many men who missed digits from fishing and construction accidents, nor known people who could maintain a professional life without a shower or indoor toilet at home. There were the itinerants, the seasonals, the locals who had left and returned and those who'd stayed, had babies, married, and divorced. There was the heels and lipstick set, which was small and drifty, and the men who lived alone in the hills who came into town lusty. People lived in all sorts of homes made out of all kinds of structures, from glamorous estates with million-dollar views to near lean-tos. There were no sub-divisions with cookie-cutter houses. One morning, one of the other teachers burst into school and shouted: "The ugliest trailer park in town is on fire. Maybe it'll finally go!" A year later, the clot of homes was razed and turned into a parking lot for the expanding community college.

This brand of diversity meant there were a number of characters around town. There were the old cranks who wrote angry letters to the editor every week. A moon-faced Japanese boy who walked all over town, always trailed by a mental health worker. A woman with a long, graying ponytail who biked everywhere in all kinds of weather. (A car accident, someone told me, had left her not quite right in the head.) There was the dwarf, a high school girl with blond hair and a silver sports car that had been tricked out to fit her.

One of my students was an eighteen-year-old girl, six feet tall and thickly built, with bugged eyes behind bottle-bottom glasses and a head of wildly curly brown hair. She had been born on an Indian reservation in the Lower 48 and had been adopted by a family who lived in the hills behind town in a modern, fortress of a house surrounded by a wide well-trimmed lawn. The girl was awkward in her movements, high-voiced, with the care-ful penmanship of a scrupulous fourth-grader, and an unpredictable intelligence. After a year, I understood her to be a young woman who had climbed out of a novel by a South American magical realist. At lunch, she whispered to me about her visions of ghosts, of chickens, of angels who flew down to touch her skin.

In a small town, there's room for everyone. Everybody needs someone worse off than themselves. But a small town is, of course, the worst place to go to hide away. People trying to escape stood out even more: those who lived far out of town and drove in only as often as they had to; those living off the road and telephone network who were contacted over the radio; people who were particularly hermitic, reclusive, or weird.

As in any small town, rumors spread like oil slicks, and people's histories trapped them like boom. Before you knew someone, you might know intimate details about their life. "She's the one who threw the glass of wine in her husband's face at the restaurant when she found out he was cheating on her." "Oh them? They're coke fiends." "He sells pain pills over the counter of his store." Domestic tangles were covered by the local newspapers, revealing more information than you thought you wanted to know about your neighbor, a friend of a friend, the guy with the backhoe you might someday need to hire. Gossip webbed the community together and sometimes felt like a trap.

Most news was good news, however. Front pages had photos of local kids skiing, performing, or catching fish. Letters to the editors were typically laudatory and formulaic: Event X Declared a Success! "And so many thanks go out to all of those who helped make this year's canned food drive possible." But there were real controversies around town: Should the city be able to annex land outside its bounds? Should the city replace the blinking red light—the only traffic signal in town—with a three-color one? Should the city let people dump fill over the bluff to shore up their disappearing properties? Growth and change brought conflicts, which played out in the local papers, in signs planted in front yards.

As the year passed, people moved in and out of town like a slow tide. In May, king salmon flushed into nearby streams and RVs followed nearly as thick. They parked in view spots, huddled close together as if for warmth. As the weather warmed, it became nearly impossible to make a left turn onto the main thoroughfare through town. You stopped at the blinking red light but never could go. The lines at the supermarket got longer, with retiree couples arriving in matching windbreakers. They looked clean, and if you hadn't been washing much yourself, they smelled clean too. Fishermen in rubber boots who were stocking up for another hitch on the water brought full carts to the cashiers loaded with the necessities: soda, chips, preformed hamburger patties, and buns.

The hotels filled up, floatplanes moved in swarms, and even the occasional private jet touched down at the airport. The bed and breakfast fad had hit Homer. Sometimes it seemed as though half the town ran a little side business in an extra bedroom. There was even a B and B in a homely yellow house on the road out of town that had an awkward painting of a moose in bedroom slippers on its front side. It was called "The Cozy Moose."

The distinction between insider and outsider played out all summer long. Visitors lingered around the public fish cleaning tables next to the harbor where locals cleaned dozens of salmon they'd netted in resident-only fisheries. "Vat kind of salmon?" a pair of spectacled Germans asked, standing out of reach of flying fish slime. "I'd be happy to take over for ya," said a gray-haired tourist from out-of-state, "just for the practice." Beneath the signs that reminded people it was illegal to sell or barter fish caught for personal use through resident fisheries, so as to not compete with commercial markets, what he meant was: I'll do a little work for you if you slip me a fillet. A gray-haired, wide-beamed man named Chris stood at the fish cleaning tables with an array of sharp knives within reach and a cigarette drooping from his lip. He charged two dollars to fillet a fish and knew when all of the charter boats returned to the harbor. In two agile sweeps of the blade, he'd pull a clean fillet off a hundred and fifty-pound halibut. Then he'd cut out the cheeks, the succulent rounds of meat on the fish's head, and toss the carcass over his shoulder into a fish dumpster, where fat gulls were waiting on the metal rim. Chris didn't live in town in the winter, but he was a fixture in the summer, and despite his grimy rubber bibs and unkempt head of gray hair, he must have been making a killing.

In late summer, the town uncluttered gradually. As the raspberries became ripe on the stalk, the fishing quieted down. The RVs headed out of town before the cranes. By the time the heavy frosts came, the traffic had thinned and the floatplane lake had quieted.

As the seasons in Alaska went by, I kept in touch with friends in other parts of the country. Suddenly, even people I'd met elsewhere and had known barely more than a year felt like old friends. Once you move so far away from anything you've known, all things familiar become dear. By then, John and I knew some other young couples. At least one or two pairs of people like us—married or not, from someplace else—seemed to drift into town each year and set anchor, at least for a while. Even so, surrounded by strangers and a looming panorama of mountains, sea, and sky, I often felt out of my element. But I wanted my element to change. "I felt now a part of the land of Alaska," is what I'd boldly written years before in my fifth-grade report. At eleven, I was unambiguous. Would these words turn out to be a prophecy?

Tom never did get that room added onto his place. But he stuck it out at the fish packing plant, returning every summer, and then later coming up for a month or so in the winter to work the Christmas rush. During the winter stints—when frozen fish was being sent all over the country but no fresh fish was coming in—the owner let him live in a small room above the cutting tables. This way, he could avoid the icy steps down to his place while helping to make sure the plant didn't get vandalized during the winter, when most of the Spit was deserted. This was no retirement plan and I wondered what would happen when Tom got too old to cut fish, to climb the stairs at his place. This was the stopgap life that so many people here subscribed to. They'd come up from someplace else to make a bundle of cash. Some would go home; others would make one here.

What I would do, I didn't know and couldn't predict. Some days I wondered how many ties I would need to stay here. Visits with Tom were nice, but they reminded me that I'd broken so many other ties to come here. And my attraction to this odd friendship—and the work of maintaining it, which I kept to myself—reminded me how love had entangled my life with John's in ways I'd never experienced before. It was at once comforting and alarming. Lately, however, I had begun to want a few more things for myself. I started taking an evening art class at the community college and playing pickup soccer a couple of nights a week. I kept my eyes out for potential friends. I needed to be connected here apart from John. I felt like the transplants that I put in my garden in the spring, the ones whose tightly bound roots I'd had to tear apart in order to help them grow new roots in the tilled bed. But you have to wait and see whether they take.

# 5

# THE RIVER'S MOUTH

RUNNING LINE: *n. A continuous line that runs between shore and a mooring buoy that allows a small craft to be moved between shore and deep water.*

This is an announcement from the Alaska Department of Fish and Game," said the man on the radio. By now, I recognized all of the station's announcers, but his voice was unfamiliar. "The Kenai River personal use dip net fishery will be open to Alaska residents at 5 A.M. on July 10 until midnight on July 31, unless closed by emergency order." Ninety miles up the highway, the Kenai twisted a wide, turquoise path from the mountains into Cook Inlet. Every summer, tourists and residents packed its banks to fish. Tourists were limited to hook and line, but over the next few weeks, hundreds of Alaskans would fish with dip nets in the glacier-fed river. These arm span–wide bags of nets were strung off solid frames with pole handles a dozen or more feet long. All over town people pulled nets out of wherever they'd been stored during the winter and spring, patched holes, strapped them to the roofs of their cars, and headed north. During these midsummer weeks, the all-around houseware, drugstore, and trinket shop prominently displayed dip nets for sale. People had been waiting all year for this.

John had set his mind on dipnetting months before. Nowhere else in the country could you fish like this. He'd heard that the red salmon you could catch up there were special; they had high oil content that made them fatty and delicious. Silver salmon—like the kind we'd caught the previous summer from the beach in front of our place—were nice, but people said that they didn't keep as well in the freezer as the reds, and the silver's pale flesh had a milder taste.

I was always eager for the next adventure John conjured up. I wanted to learn something new, experience something different, go to a place I'd never been before. But as John schemed, I floundered. Where could we find the equipment? What day should we go? How did it all work? We didn't know much about how fishing was done up there, but we knew we needed nets and waterproof chest waders so that we could stand in the river holding the nets out as the fish ran upstream. But we couldn't afford to buy the nets and waders new, and used gear was usually passed from friend to friend to friend.

John's mind was set: We would go. He started looking for ways to borrow equipment or otherwise get it for free. He was good at this. A few days later, Cynthia, our friend who lived in the yurt, asked us if we wanted to go with her. She had borrowed two nets and two pairs of waders from her neighbors and would share them with us. Her husband, Taro, was out of town, commercial fishing for salmon at the mouth of the Copper River about two hundred miles east by boat.

Cynthia was in her mid-thirties, nearly ten years older than I, and she had become my closest friend. I didn't think she'd ever understand the accumulation of my inabilities, but I felt close to her anyway because she had a secret sweet tooth, despite an otherwise wholesome diet, and because of the way she seemed to hold within her, as I did within myself, the desire to talk about things that often went unsaid. From time to time she would ask me to cut her curly brown hair. I would pull a stool into the middle of the kitchen, wrap a towel around her shoulders, and snip curls inexpertly, until they were all a few inches shorter but no less wild.

The five of us—John and I, and Cynthia and her children Kaya and Ghen—would go up together that Saturday. The kids, now seven and five, would stay on the beach while we took turns fishing. We checked the tide tables to figure out when to head up to the river. Cynthia, who had fished there before, said that we should plan to arrive before high tide and stay until it was nearly low tide. Because the river's mouth opened farther up Cook Inlet than our bay, the tides were about two hours later there than they were in Homer. Cynthia and the kids pulled up to our place before 8:00 A.M. The day was overcast. We strapped the nets to the roof of John's car—a ten-year-old Jeep he'd bought off someone in town when he realized that his old Volvo wasn't much good in the snow. We packed lunches, snacks, and water, fastened the kids' seat belts, threw the waders in the back and took off.

The drive up the highway was one we, like everyone else in Homer, were familiar with. It was the only way out of town, the only route to Anchorage and to a medium-sized town along the way that was primarily a strip of gas stations, fast-food restaurants, and souvenir stores. Though it wasn't much more populated than Homer, people drove up there anyway to shop at an enormous supermarket where you could buy everything from winter boots and California oranges to clam shovels, underwear, and kitchen tables. West, to our left, a string of volcanic peaks stretched along the far side of the Inlet. On clear days, from town, you could often see the two highest peaks letting out dainty puffs of steam. Along the right side of the road, stunted spruce grew at the edges of bogs and around small lakes. A tiny espresso stand had sprung up just before the bridge over a narrow, clear-running river, and houses intermittently dotted the edge of the highway. When the trees broke to our east, we could see the northern arm of the range of mountains that curved around the bay.

After a little over an hour in the car, John turned left off the highway onto a road that bowed out along the shore of the Inlet. Spruce- and birch-flanked driveways led to hidden houses off the paved road. A few miles later, we made another left onto a gravel road down to the beach. The Inlet opened up in front of us. The snowy peaks across the water scraped a high, white ceiling of clouds. The sea looked gray and cold. Small waves purled down the beach. John put the Jeep into four-wheel drive and drove it off a wide parking pad onto a well-rutted track in the beach. The back end of the car swung sideways as it lost traction in the soft sand. The kids were beginning to fidget in the backseat. They craned their heads to look out the windows because they knew we were almost there. Up ahead, a clutter of trucks and cars parked on the beach.

As we approached the mouth of the river, a haphazard encampment came into view. Scores of cars and trucks were parked on the beach near the edge of sandy dunes. Among them, people had pitched colorful tents that were ringed by coolers, tubs of gear, beach chairs, campfires, and stacks of firewood. Clothes hung from makeshift lines strung between driftwood poles and dogs barked from where they were tied up at the camps. John parked the car next to a large pickup that sat diagonally on the beach. As we got out, the smell hit me—a combination of fish, piss, and smoky campfires that was wafting down the beach. It appeared that entire families had relocated for a day or the weekend, or longer. All along the beach at the mouth of the river, hundreds of people stood waist-deep in the river with the handles of their nets stretched out in front of them. Kids ran between the water's edge and their families' territories on the beach. A cluster of women sat talking and smoking cigarettes on folding chairs in front of the grill of an oversize pickup. Men, taking a break from the river, stood around with the tops of their waders folded down to the waist. Trucks and ATVs fishtailed down the beach in a steady stream and parked in the sand.

We undid the nets from the roof of the car. Cynthia offered to stay on the beach with the kids, so John and I put the waders on over our pants and long-sleeved shirts. These waterproof overalls were heavy but supple, with shoulder straps and attached rubber boots. It was a cool summer day, and it was always colder on the beach as wind swept off the Inlet's fifty-five-degree water to shore. I watched as John walked into the water ahead of me with his net outstretched and perpendicular to the river's bottom. He casually greeted the man standing in the river a few feet in front of him. I carried my net to the edge of the water and then waded into the river, trying to keep the net upright in front of me. I inched it forward until it fell over, then I picked it up and started again. Shoving the circular frame of net along the sandy river bottom, I continued into the river until I was aligned with John and the handle of my net stretched toward the center of the river. Already John was adjusting how he held his net by observing the people around us. I did the same and rested the handle on my left shoulder and held it there with my hand. In the river up to my sternum, I shifted around to stand comfortably, feet spread, both hands gripping the end of the net's handle to keep it upright. John asked the man next to him how the fishing had been earlier that morning.

"Nothing to speak of but they hit pretty good last night, 'bout ten o'clock," the man reported. "My wife's got a full cooler," he said, tipping his head toward the top of the beach where, I assumed, his wife sat with the fish. They continued to talk about fishing, the timing of that day's tides, whether the commercial boats had an opener and were allowed to extend their nets in the Inlet to intercept fish on their way to the river's mouth.

"See all them drifters out there?" the man motioned beyond the mouth of the river toward the Inlet where nearly a dozen commercial fishing boats with large spools in their sterns lined up on the horizon. We were vultures, all of us, circling.

The cold water pressed heavily against me. It was a delicious feeling being held by the river like that. The water buoyed me up and squeezed me. It did not chuck me out. Slack high tide had filled the river's mouth with seawater—a zealous gulp that swelled the channel far beyond its bounds and would later be spit back out.

No one was catching any fish, despite the fact that there were scores of people in the water and crowding the beach. We stood there anyway, a few feet apart from one another, holding our dip nets extending toward the middle of the river. These nets looked like giant versions of the green, foot-long nets used to scoop goldfish out of an aquarium. The dip net's fine filament caught a fish behind its gills, or simply tangled it in the bag of net. Around me, people were using all sorts of homemade nets. A man nearby had fashioned his handle out of a bicycle handlebar. Another had used a crutch. Some homemade nets had been made with long pieces of PVC pipe, which sagged, or copper tubing, which was a little bit more rigid. Other people had extra-sturdy nets they'd welded from aluminum pipe; some had bought nets ready-made. Duct tape patched many of the nets, and a few people had attached empty, capped soda bottles to the top of the mouth of their nets, which provided a little bit of buoyancy on one side of the net to help keep it upright in the water. Our borrowed nets were made from welded aluminum pipe, and knots in the netting revealed many seasons of use. Here was a scene I had come to realize was typical—a mix of do-it-yourself, scavenged parts, failing equipment, and industrial-strength engineering.

I looked down the line of people standing in the river and scanned back across the beach. Everyone was waiting, as in some modern myth in which the prospect of a flood of fish brought every kind of person to this sandy shore that would be—for a day at least—our ark. I was surrounded by people of every race, age, and description. We were only a three-hour drive from Anchorage, where the majority of dipnetters came from, and we were close to a half dozen or so small towns. Here was a diversity of people I'd never seen before in Alaska. There were young urbanites who had come in SUVs, and scruffy types who looked as though this was their first public outing since the same time last summer. There were white, Asian, and black families, and groups of Russian Old Believers, a sect of Russian Orthodox who lived in secluded communities scattered across the region. The women wore long, pastel dresses even on the beach, and the bearded men stood in the water with the high collars of their embroidered shirts sticking up above their waders. There were military families with clean-shaven and close-cropped fathers and people fishing by themselves. There were seniors and kids, wading into the water wearing jeans, and all ages in between.

Dipnetting began here in the early 1980s as a way to encourage people to skim what managers saw as an overabundance of salmon from the rivers. Salmon runs left to their own devices fluctuated naturally, too widely for commercial fishermen, who wanted a reliable harvest. Years when the river was thick with fish would be followed by lulls; a mass of fish hatching in the river might strip it bare of food, meaning fewer smolt made it out to sea where they became adults and got ready to head back upriver. So dipnetting was initiated to cull salmon from the river before they could spawn, thereby thinning what could become an overpopulation of fish. This, managers believed, would help ensure that commercial fishing for these salmon was as productive as possible. In the beginning, dipnetting was only allowed after the commercial boats were assured a full harvest. If there weren't "extra" fish, no one could dipnet. But over the years, the activity became more popular and gained higher-priority status. These days, people could start dipnetting on July 10 every year, and didn't need to wait until the commercial boats got their fill. And sometimes, when low salmon returns halted commercial fishing, dipnetters would still be busy pulling fish in from shore.

Although this dipnet fishery was a little more than twenty years old, standing in the edge of the river among the enthusiastic throngs of people, I felt part of an ancient ritual of harvest. And we were, of course, repeating what had been done in these waters for countless years. Dip nets had been around long before people figured out how to make them out of aluminum and spare parts.

Everyone was waiting—for the next fish, for the tide to turn, to reach their catch limit so they could go home. No one knew when the fish would begin to move up the river—or even whether that day they would at all. But people knew enough to stick around until the tide began to retreat, bringing fresh water once again down the river, cuing the salmon to move upstream. As the minutes ebbed with no fish, people dragged their nets out of the water and waited on land. People sat on coolers, went back to their camps and warmed up by the fire, sprawled on tarps to nap, ate fried chicken someone had picked up at a nearby fast-food restaurant. This wasn't wilderness. We could see fish processing buildings along the bank of the river farther upstream, and commercial fishing boats came up the river, trailing wakes that fanned out to shore and swamped your waders if you weren't paying attention.

A LITTLE WHILE after high tide, the sea turned back. The Inlet's gray water began to pull strongly against us, and my arms started to ache from the strain of holding the net upright against the current. John and I were standing in the river as shouts began to fly up around us. A woman a few yards down the beach ran up the sand dragging her net behind her. A salmon as long as my arm jerked in her net. "Got one!" the man next to John called out before heading out of the water. Down the line of dipnetters, people began jogging out of the river with their nets. "They're here!" someone announced. The fish had hit. John hollered to me as he waded out of the water with a salmon in his net. I felt a thud in my net and then flipped it flat against the river's sandy bottom. The weight disappeared. "I lost it!" I shouted to John. "Turn your net downstream," he called out as he untangled the fish from his net and carried it up the beach to where Cynthia and the kids were sitting on the sand. Everyone around me was catching fish; I was dying to catch my own. A moment later, I felt the thud again and rotated the net downriver until it was flat. I waded out of the water as fast as I could, dragging the net behind me. As the mouth of the net emerged from the water, I could see what had been thrashing in it: my first Kenai River red salmon. It was a few inches longer than the silver salmon we had caught the previous summer and weighed about ten pounds. Fresh from the sea, its bright silver skin darkened to a deep blue-green along the back, and its sleek body hadn't yet started to contort into its spawning form.

I left the fish with Cynthia and the kids, and as I was rushing back into the water, John came out with another red in his net. All around us, people cheered in excitement as they felt that particular tug of fish pulling against their nets. I let out a surprised yelp as one bumped against my submerged thighs.

A man in a plaid shirt and baseball cap a few spots down from me pulled his net out to find a flounder the size of a platter. "That's a nice size," his neighbor said. "You gonna keep that?"

"Na. These things are mush. Even my dog won't eat 'em." And before his neighbor could ask for it, he threw it back into the river.

When the pull of the retreating tide and the river's current became so strong it was nearly impossible to hold our nets upright in the river, the line of people at the edge of the water began to move downstream with the flow of water like a conveyor belt. John and I followed. Once we got a few hundred yards down the beach, we would pull our nets out of the water and hike back up the beach to the mouth of the river and wade out again. With the tide going out, the river was narrowing and the edge of the water migrated down the beach. Sand sucked out from beneath my boots. We trailed along, always staying about chest-deep with our nets stretched toward the center of the river. Beyond the edges of our nets, a man and woman in wet suits and flippers were floating downstream holding dip nets afloat in front of them. Smiling, they waved at us on shore and we waved back. When they reached the mouth of the river, they got out of the water, slowly walked up the beach in their awkward footwear, and started the process again. But there was hardly a need to go anywhere. A minute after John and I put our nets back into the water, we each caught another fish. A man in front of me caught two reds in his net at once. The gray sea suddenly seemed full of life and a constant rush of footprints turned over the surface of the beach.

Being immersed in such an excess of fish was dazzling. They were being drawn out of the milky gray water all around me. We couldn't see the fish, but knew they had to be there in the thousands, moving upstream together toward their spawning ground. I felt a strange kind of mania when the fish came in thickly like that, creating a new kind of hunger in me. I couldn't feel that water had gotten into my waders and dribbled down my right leg to pool in my boot. I didn't notice that my arms were drenched past the elbow. I couldn't feel that muscles in my torso were working in ways they never had.

As we moved along the beach, a small skiff packed with a half-dozen people zipped by just beyond the edge of our nets. The passengers each held a dip net that dragged through the water, combing out fish. Every time the skiff passed us, the passengers dropped more fish into the boat's hull.

Ecstatic cheers went up as a small, gray-haired Asian woman dragged her net onto the beach. An enormous king salmon—about thirty pounds—bucked in her net. It was late for this kind of salmon to be running up the river and it was beginning to look a little bit "spawny"—losing its silver brilliance, turning pink, and gaining hook-shaped jaws. But that didn't matter. People clapped and the woman's family crowded around her.

We continued to ferry fish to Cynthia and the kids on the beach—one, two, six, a dozen. All three of them sat on the sand removing the guts but they couldn't keep up with us. After pulling in a few more fish, I took off the waders and joined the kids on the beach, while Cynthia headed into the water.

One of our three coolers was full of cleaned fish, and a few other reds lay twitching in the sand next to a pile of guts. We had no ice, but these fish were fresher than any you could find in the best markets. Kaya and Ghen were excited. At seven, Kaya had an unusually keen sense of observation. She watched half in awe and half in disgust as a boy about her age was vigorously hitting a salmon flopping on the beach with a small wooden club. A sharp smack stunned the fish so that it could be easily untangled from the net. But the boy's blows were failing to still the fish. By some measures, it was a violent scene for a child to witness. But sentimentality quickly gave way to practicality. "Why doesn't he just rip its gills?" Kaya asked. "That would work better." I had looked up from the fish I was preparing to slit open and briefly wondered why it was so easy to surround myself with so much killing, why it was so easy to enjoy it. It seemed there should be some ritual of appreciation before we all drove off the beach lugging these tons of fish home, some kind of celebration to mark the sacrifice, but there was far too much work to do as the fish continued to stream in. The fish would be our food and also a kind of currency. It would provide gifts to send to family out of state; meals we gave to older neighbors, unable to fish themselves; and dinners to be shared on winter nights with friends. At that moment, nothing was more important than the harvest.

PEOPLE HERE WERE always gathering things. Coal was collected from the beaches to heat houses. Driftwood—from small, sinuous pieces to huge trunks of redwood—was taken from the dunes for construction and art, until a city mandate forbade it to protect the beach from erosion. Still, people hauled away heavy tree trunks that washed ashore each year. People collected sand to add to garden beds or to scatter across icy front steps. People took stones for their yards and to weigh down the backs of their trucks for traction in the snow. Dead trees were leveled to feed woodstoves. Water was piped off streams for the garden or from a spring to the kitchen tap. Nothing edible was ignored.

In a way, this sense of abundance reminded me of my childhood. The strip of woods on the far side of the creek behind my parents' house was the source of all the raw materials my friends and I needed for a Saturday afternoon. But as I'd grown older, few things seemed free anymore. And there was so little raw material left at my disposal. Adult life seemed circumscribed by scarcity: never enough money, enough time, enough happiness. "Excess" had become a pejorative. But here, at this time of year, it was hard to feel anything but rich with the profusion of resources here. A few weeks earlier, John and I had dug dozens of long, thin-shelled razor clams from the Inlet's muddy shores during a particularly low tide, and we collected steamer clams and mussels across the bay. Gardens were beginning to fill out all over town; people were picking radishes, greens, and their first broccoli heads. King salmon had already run up some of the local rivers. People were pulling the last packages of moose meat from their freezers to make room for fish. Potluck dinners felt extravagant: clam chowder; moose ribs, halibut, and salmon fillets for the grill; smoked salmon of all kinds; octopus salad. Each shared dish represented so much effort, its own story, a recipe perfected by years of tinkering and passing around. The bounty was staggering.

And yet the abundance of resources had been changing. Those days, the main commercial fisheries in the region were for salmon, halibut, cod, and herring. But what was harvested for profit and for the pantry had changed drastically over the years. By the late 1920s, when a handful of homesteads had been staked out around Homer, twenty herring salteries hummed busily on the south shore of Kachemak Bay. Soon after, the foot-long silver fish that were caught by net when they came to shore by the millions to spawn disappeared. They had been over-fished, and their spawning grounds had been ruined by offal from fish packing plants. Although no commercial herring fishery has existed in the bay since then, fishermen still net them up Cook Inlet. A stable shrimp industry once existed in the bay. Using nets and trawls, fishermen

harvested shrimp commercially until the fishery went
bust in the mid–1980s. These days, the most readily available shrimp were from farms in Southeast Asia and came
in one- or two-pound frozen packages at the warehouse
grocery store. People around town talked about the time,
as recent as the mid-1980s, when you could wade off the
tip of the Spit during low tide and pull a king crab with
two-foot-long legs out of the bay. Now, there were no
king crabs to be found. Tanner and Dungeness crabs,
smaller but tasty species, had also been harvested commercially in the bay, but these fisheries had been shut
down too. A few years before John and I moved to town,
people would drop crab pots off the ferry dock on the tip
of the Spit to catch a few Dungies for dinner. Because of
scarcity, this too was now forbidden.

Researchers attributed the fluctuation in fisheries to
something called "regime change," which referred to long-
term cycles in weather, ocean currents, and temperatures.
The regime, they said, had shifted from shellfish—crab
and shrimp—to finfish, namely salmon and halibut. A
local scientist, however, had found that a few of the region's rivers had gotten warmer in recent years, making
conditions less favorable for salmon. People were beginning to suspect the rivers were getting warmer for good,
and it was clear that fishing regulations could only do so
much. They might be able to save a single season of fish or
protect a faltering market, but they couldn't bring back the
past, couldn't stem the hunger, couldn't stop the oceans
from changing in ways no one could fully understand. But

standing in the river, we didn't think about any of this. It seemed that this run of red salmon would last forever.

This sense—that almost nothing could be used up— gripped the state. There were no contingency plans for when the oil and gas tap dried up, and regulations on development were lax and enforcement was even laxer. There were always so many more wetlands, so many more miles of shoreline, and so many trees, that individual transgressions often went overlooked.

And Alaska's plenitude fed the hunger; its resources were hankered for all over the world. Japan took the state's natural gas. China bought Alaska's raw logs. Taiwan sought the state's coal and Mexico bought fertilizer made out of Alaska's natural gas. Canada dug its silver, zinc, and lead, and Alaska's seafood was snatched up all over the world: choice king crab in Japan, pink salmon in Korea, and halibut and cod in Germany.

We all were romanced by this sense of bounty. Even people who considered themselves conservationists didn't think twice about scraping a level pad in order to build a house on land that had no other marks of human contact. We collected clams and mussels—which were not restricted by regulations—whenever we could without regard for scarcity. On the biggest days during the weeks of dipnetting on the Kenai, fifty, sixty, sometimes seventy thousand fish pushed upriver in a single day. Whole fish piled up in the Anchorage landfill during the peak of dipnetting, dumped there by people who'd brought home more than they could handle. We took anything we could, enough for now and plenty for later. Perhaps this is what it felt like in the rest of America before the commons were commodified, before our own hunger hemmed us in.

JOHN AND CYNTHIA continued to ferry flopping salmon over to where the kids and I sat in the sand. All down the beach, people were gutting fish on whatever surface they could find. Some worked on the sand, while others used the lids of coolers until blood dripped down the sides. Others had carted down pieces of plywood or light folding tables. There were even a few ironing boards standing on the beach. Kids ran around with buckets collecting roe that people chucked onto the sand when they cleaned fish. The fish eggs could be cured for bait or eaten fried, salted, or prepared in many other ways. Although I hated to waste anything edible, the eggs were fishy and gelatinous and with pounds of beautiful salmon fillets in our future, I had no interest in keeping them.

In the middle of the chaos, Kaya and Ghen were thrilled. Ghen danced around the dying fish, and when John ran over with another, I ripped its gills to kill and bleed it and then asked the kids to help me clean it. I first clipped the tips of the tail off the salmon with a pair of scissors we had brought with us. As with the restrictions on gillnetting for personal use, the law required us to mark the fish in this way to ensure these fish wouldn't dilute the already struggling commercial salmon market.

Around me, people had tied scissors gunked up with blood, slime, and sand onto cooler handles so they wouldn't get lost on the beach. The chances of getting caught were minimal but the risk—losing the ability to dipnet—was too great. I took a short knife and sliced the salmon's belly, tail to head. The kids reached their hands inside the body and pulled out multicolored innards and tossed them onto the gut pile. I slid my hand inside and scraped the tips of my fingers against the backbone to clean out the bloodline. I could feel the ribs under a thin layer of slick tissue. Then I reached up toward its head and pulled out the heart. I unfolded my hand in front of the kids to show the grape-sized organ pulsing against my palm. They squealed with delight and each took turns feeling the shudder of the heart against their skin.

BY THE TIME we had nearly three dozen fish, the tide had receded far down the beach. All around us was a carnal scene of death and destruction. Fish guts and blood littered the beach, graying in the open air. A wrack of fish heads had formed at the water's edge. A slurry of blood and fish slime pooled in the bottom of the coolers. Gulls swarmed as thick as gnats, fighting over fish heads and guts, though the beach was thick with it all. "I never hated seagulls before," a woman cleaning fish nearby said. She had camped on the beach the night before and been kept awake by the birds' incessant cries. There were no out-houses so people stole off into the dunes, leaving a rank mess. People cleaning fish for their families had lost hope of keeping up with those catching them. In their haste, people often discarded strips of belly meat because they contained small fins that were difficult to remove. This was the fattest part of the meat, succulent and oily, and white-skinned curls of flesh lay scattered across the sand.

It felt at once like a massacre and a celebration. When the fish were coming up the river in large numbers, everyone was excited, talkative, and helpful. There was more than enough fish for everyone, and we'd have it all winter long. It was this sense of plenty that was beginning to tie me tightly to the life here and make me wonder if I could ever leave.

The more I learned about this particular way of life, the more rooted I felt. I learned the unspoken rules about harvesting wild foods. You would tell people about the spot where you'd had good fishing luck but not about the wild blueberry patch you'd found on a hike. Nobody hoarded fish; it was what you shared. And you had to be creative about how you put up your fish. While Kenai River red salmon fillets carefully packed and frozen were tastier than what was sold at upscale markets in East Coast cities for nearly twenty dollars a pound, people didn't think twice about stuffing salmon steaks—bones and skin and all—into glass jars and blasting them with higher-than-boiling-point heat for over an hour in a pressure canner. Once they had cooled, you could stack them in your pantry where they would keep for years. What you didn't can or freeze could be pickled, smoked, and salted. John and I had learned some things through our mistakes, such as how salmon fillets vacuum-packed and flash-frozen by the plant on the Spit always lasted longer in the freezer than if we packed and froze it ourselves.

NEARLY TWO HOURS later, the fishing had slowed. It was almost slack low tide, and the original surge of freshwater that had triggered the salmon to run upstream was long past. We had about three dozen fish. Although by law we could take many more—twenty-five for each head of a household and ten for every other family member— we had enough. John and Cynthia came back from the water's edge, nets balanced on their shoulders. Cynthia dropped hers to the sand. Her wide, pale face was lit with excitement and exhaustion. "Beautiful fish!" she cheered. John beamed quietly. This, I knew, was what he'd dreamed of in moving here. As with me, the day had made him feel useful and strong, self-sufficient and resourceful. He felt this as deeply as he felt birds: the deep soul-satisfaction of a day well lived. John, Cynthia, the kids and I—something had come alive inside us in the midst of it all. For us, work was play. Survival and leisure commingled.

All around us, people were cleaning and packing up fish. At the water's edge we rinsed each salmon—its belly sliced open and its head still on—and rinsed the coolers free of blood, slime, and sand. We packed all the fish back into the coolers. It took two of us to lift each one into the back of the car. As we loaded up the rest of the gear, I could feel the exhaustion settling into my body. My arms were so tired, I couldn't make a fist. On the drive home, only John, who was at the wheel, didn't doze off.

I woke up the next morning with the weight of exhaustion still in my muscles. Cynthia brought over the kids and a sharp, Japanese knife around noon and we laid the fish out on the grass next to the picnic table: thirty-three red salmon, cleaned, but with the heads on. For hours we stood at the table filleting the fish. We pressed our knives into the fish behind the head, down to the backbone, and then across the side of the fish to the tail, slicing the flesh free from the spine. Cynthia kept some heads to make soup stock, and we stacked the backbones which still held small bits of flesh against the ribs off to one side. Scales glittered like sequins across the table's grayed wood top, and from time to time we rinsed everything clean with a garden hose until the silver flecks dripped into the grass.

By late afternoon, when we had finished the last fish, we were exhausted and hungry. Soon we would drive the coolers of fillets out to the Spit where we'd wait on line behind tourists just off charter halibut trips to have our fish packed and flash-frozen. They'd look in awe at the piles of deep red fillets we'd hand over to the packing plant for pickup in a day or so. For less than a dollar per pound, this frozen fish would last us well into March. But before we took off, we could think of nothing but taking a break and stemming our hunger. We put a few backbones on a cookie sheet and broiled them briefly in the oven. When we took them out, the meat was cooked and glistened with fish oil. The muscle along the ribs and spine clutched the bones in tasty strands. We gathered around the tray and picked the meat off with our fingers.

# 6

# ON THE WATER

CONFUSED SEA: *n. A highly disturbed water surface without a single, well-defined direction of wave travel which may follow a sudden shift in wind direction.*

D o you think it's too rough?" I asked John. We looked out across the water from the cobble beach at the tip of the Spit. We were standing in rubber boots, waterproof pants, and raincoats on a sunny summer evening. In an unpaved parking lot at the top of the beach, the Jeep sat with a double kayak strapped to the roof and two days' worth of food and camping gear in the back. We were planning to paddle across the bay—a four-mile crossing—to camp for a couple of nights, but, knowing that we couldn't gauge the conditions of the sea unless we were at the water's edge, we looked out onto the surface, trying to decide whether it was safe to make the crossing.

It was nearly nine o'clock; the bay should have already lay down. Instead, the water had a small chop; I didn't like the look of it. I was scared of paddling across unless the bay was glassy. I wanted so badly for John to say we shouldn't go.

"It looks OK to me," he said. "What about you?"

The gravel shifted under my feet. "Yeah, yeah. I guess it's okay," I managed. I stared across at a cluster of rocky islands called Gull Rocks, where thousands of seabirds nested each summer. Once we reached them, I would be close to protected water and could relax. It wouldn't take that long, I told myself, only about an hour.

"You checked the forecast, right?" I asked.

"Winds to five knots. No big deal."

"Do you think it's okay?" I asked again.

He looked at me. He knew I wanted him to decide, to tell me either that everything would be fine, or that we shouldn't go. He resisted. "Let's make this decision together. Are you comfortable with this?"

I knew I could say no, that we could drive home and try again in the morning. But John was willing to go. I didn't want to be the one to hold us back.

It was only a few weeks past summer solstice, so the evening sunlight was strong, picking out the whites of gulls and murres on the water. Although Kachemak Bay was fairly protected, wind could pick up at any moment and rile the surface of the sea. Tankers rumbled in and out of the bay, and droves of charter and commercial fishing boats left imposing wakes across the water.

We had paddled across the bay twice earlier that summer, both times leaving in the early morning, when the water was flat and glassy. The bay's surface was typically smooth at this time, before the sun had warmed the air over the land, making it rise, and stirring up the day breeze. I felt fairly comfortable paddling when the water lay smooth and cleanly reflected the mountain range on the other side. I liked the sea to be silent, the tide slack, and the sky static and dull. But even then, out in the middle of the bay, half an hour from land on either side, I felt that just the depth of the sea could pull me down.

Few people crossed the bay in kayaks, though they'd been designed thousands of years ago as sturdy, seagoing hunting craft. These slim, low-profile boats, originally made from skins stretched over wood frames, were light and stable in the water. Many of the modern versions had foot-controlled rudders for easier steering. And these boats had enough storage space to pack a week's worth of gear. Rather than make the crossing in kayaks, most people rented kayaks from one of the outfits on the south shore or went on guided paddling trips offered during the summer. Even among locals who owned their own kayaks, most hired water taxis to take them into the more protected inlets and fjords on the other side of the bay. But people did paddle across, usually young, experienced sea kayakers with the holds of their boats packed for a few nights of camping.

John was an experienced paddler. A few years before, he had built his own wooden sea kayak, a sleek, seventeen-foot craft of plywood as thin as two stacked nickels, with fiberglass and epoxy to make it strong and watertight. He had grown up near Washington State's Puget

Sound and had been in and out of boats for years. As we set out to explore our new home together, my inexperience with the sea betrayed me. But this was my home and I wanted to explore it. If you didn't get out on the water, you missed so much.

The past winter, John had sent off for a kit so that we could build a boat for me like the one he had built for himself. The kit arrived in two boxes by truck, and we laid out the plywood pieces on the basement floor. It was a puzzle: Two spear-shaped sections for the deck would be joined at the cockpit and trimmed to size. Four plywood blades would form the hull. Wooden pentagons would become bulkheads, and rib-shaped pieces would be used to trim and strengthen. Everything was flat. Over the next few months, we drilled tiny holes into the pale wood and then stitched the plywood pieces together with copper wire. Winter was a perfect time for this kind of extended project, but I often didn't feel like descending into the cold basement to work on it. The project required a kind of patience and strict attention to detail I lacked. One mismeasure, I feared, and I would ruin the entire boat. But John coaxed me through it, showing me how to use a plane, mix epoxy, make a joint. As the light began to return in late winter, we articulated the craft; the boat gained dimension like a pile of bones articulated back into its skeleton. I came to love the deck, with the camber of a thigh, and the hard chine of the hull, which would help keep me upright.

I did the finishing work alone that spring, spending hour after hour sanding and varnishing until the hull and deck shone flawlessly. I lay tape midway down the hull on either side of the boat, then painted the wood creamy white between the lines. If I overturned on the bay, the white stripe would be more visible to passing boats than a wood-brown hull. When I finished, John and I carried the boat down the bluff to the gravel beach. Gentle waves unraveled across the bow, and John held the kayak steady as I stepped in. Then he lifted the stern and shoved me off. On the boat's maiden voyage, I paddled close to shore, slicing the gleaming craft through murky water. Narrow in beam, the kayak held me closely at my hips and responded gracefully to my strokes. It fit me perfectly and felt like mine.

I hoped that having my own boat would fortify me against the fear I felt on the water. I was terrified of the sea at the same time I was drawn to it. Half an hour from land, I would freeze. Suddenly, the blue depth of the bay was an incessant and distracting mystery. How many fathoms of water lay below us? What was down there? The sun shafted into the ocean, but those pillars of light dissipated in the darkness.

SHOULD WE GO? I asked myself. My hands dug into the pockets of my raincoat where sand had collected in the seams. I was relieved we had decided to leave our own wooden boats at home and borrow a double kayak for the trip. We'd paddled it before and knew the heavy boat was more stable in the water, better for less-than-ideal paddling conditions. John would take the stern, controlling our direction, and from the bow, the bay would stretch unbroken in front of me. I felt safer having him close; it was easy to get out of earshot paddling separately. But having only one boat meant that if we tipped, we both went in.

I looked across the bay. Patches of snow near the peaks of the mountains glowed under the sun. The only way to get over my fear was to force myself into situations that scared me. But the small chop on the bay that evening was the roughest we'd ever considered paddling through.

I had realized there was nothing you could count on about the sea. Mornings, the bay was usually glassy, but not always. Evenings, the sea would usually lie down, but not always. Such unpredictability meant that there were so many precautions to take and things to consider. Life was like that here. If you weren't prepared for every possibility, you weren't prepared. And this wasn't just the case on the water. Hiking on the trails outside of town, you watched for bears and paid attention to the weather. When paddling, you zipped a cigarette lighter into your life vest pocket—and maybe an energy bar, too—in case you got stranded. You carried water, safety equipment, extra clothes. On the water, the sea conspired with the sky. The wind could pick up from any direction, and the bay's temperature in the summer hovered around fifty degrees. You had to study the map, keep track of the weather, and listen to what people were saying. "It's starting to pick up out there. Front coming in." And then you had to decide whether to stay or to go.

It was common on these sunny summer days for the bay to froth with whitecaps and rise up in five- to eight-foot waves by the afternoon. And although the bay didn't open directly onto the Gulf of Alaska, wind could sweep up it, teasing waves off its surface. The bay was only forty miles long, but southwesterlies had a hundred miles of uninterrupted sea—called fetch—to build before reaching the mouth. "Small craft advisories" went out over the radio when sustained winds above eighteen knots were predicted and the seas grew to four feet or more. People waited out these conditions before crossing the bay in small skiffs.

Midway between the lulls of highs and lows, tides ripped around the tip of the Spit, around rock promontories, and out of narrow inlets, breaking glassy water into unpredictable shards. The day breeze could pick up at any moment. Even in isolated fjords, cold winds sweeping off the ice field could rake waves off otherwise protected waters. And when the tide was high, it was often hard to find a place to land boats.

Cold water kills fast. In the bay, at its summer temperature, you could last for half an hour to an hour before complete exhaustion or unconsciousness. After one to three hours in this water, you would likely die. Bodies lose heat twenty-five times faster in cold water than in cold air. And as your temperature drops, your heart slows and your breathing becomes less frequent. Extreme cold makes people confused and irrational. Those suffering from severe hypothermia often reject help, insisting that they're fine. Sometimes they feel an overwhelming desire to undress.

All year long, people died in Alaska's waterways—averaging nearly one per week. Some died from fishing accidents: a line knotting itself around the ankle of a young deckhand and carrying him down, or a fisherman crushed between boat and dock. Others drowned when their boats went down in rough seas. Although commercial and recreational fishing had gotten much safer than in past decades, pleasure boating killed nearly twenty people each year, which meant that water was twenty times more likely to kill you than a bear. Locals and tourists alike died in lakes, rivers, and off the coast. The sea was particularly cold, volatile, and ruthless.

All around us was evidence of past disasters. Everyone knew of someone who had lost a loved one at sea. At a bar in town one night, a man told me, "Every year it used to be that some drunks would grab a rowboat at the tip of the Spit and try to get across the bay. It was an easy way to die." Out near the end of the Spit, a bronze statue of a fisherman—rubber bibs and boots, a line in his hand—paid homage to those lost at sea, and each spring, at the start of the commercial fishing season, a crowd gathered around this Seafarer's Memorial for the blessing of the fleet. A bridge up the highway was named after a man who drowned in the river below it during an annual canoeing competition twenty-five years ago. That year, the event was abolished.

In Southcentral Alaska, where we lived, the sea could

be especially ornery. The two-hundred-mile-long Cook Inlet into which our bay opened was pushed and pulled by the largest tides in the country: The difference between the heights of high and low tides could be as much as thirty feet. This meant that extreme tides barreled into narrow arms of the Inlet on a wave called the tidal bore. This wall of water could be as high as six feet and race fifteen miles per hour. Signs along the highway that edged the Inlet's coast warned people not to wander into the mudflats that were exposed at low tide. You could get stuck as the tide rushed back in.

During winter's coldest weather, ice formed on the Inlet. There might be a greasy-looking layer of slush that undulated with the surface of the sea. Sometimes pancakes of ice floated on the Inlet's surface and then collided and froze together in floes that could be a quarter-mile wide. These dynamic conditions and the presence of sandbars that shifted invisibly under the cloudy water made Cook Inlet's shipways some of the most dangerous in the world. Law required that boat pilots knowledgeable in local conditions navigate container ships and tankers entering and leaving the Inlet. Helicopters brought pilots out to ships waiting near the mouth of the bay; tugboats ferried other pilots, who lived in Homer and other nearby towns, from the tip of the Spit to ships anchored in the bay. From shore, we'd watch the tugs approach, stop along the starboard or port side momentarily, and then return to the harbor. Soon after, the large ship would exit the bay.

Even with these precautions, accidents still happened.

Oil tankers had been ripped repeatedly from fueling docks by ice rushing out the Inlet on receding tides. Ice tore pilings out from under an oil dock and sealed a freighter's water intake valve, causing it to lose power and drift. Some people thought that the conditions were ripe for the next devastating oil spill.

It wasn't just the sea that was volatile. At the base of the Spit, a blue sign with the white silhouette of a wave pointed east along a road that led out of town to higher elevation: the tsunami evacuation route. And every Thursday at noon, the tsunami siren wailed out its test. We knew it could happen. Here, along the Ring of Fire, where a string of volcanoes puffed away across Cook Inlet, and the oceanic plate was being forced beneath a restless and fragmented continental plate, almost anything could.

The Earth. The sea. The very things we depended on could slap us and take us down. It was unnerving. What made this area geologically rich also made it volatile. What made the sea beautiful and productive also made it deadly.


"YES. LET'S GO," I said to John. Those words set us both into wordless action. We heaved the double kayak off the roof of the car and carried it in two goes to the water's edge. We unpacked the gear from the back of the car and toted it down to the boat. Sleeping bags and pads, tent, stove, food, warm clothes—everything had been packed in waterproof bags. We lowered them, piece by piece, into the kayak's bow and stern. John had already put on his life vest and spray skirt, which kept water from getting into the cockpit, by the time I reached for my purple vest. I pressed my hand against a zipped pocket on the vest: The lighter was there. John was looking out on the water. He was always like that—looking, observing, noting every bird, watching the movement of the tide, and scanning for skiffs he recognized. The wind had picked up slightly. After I pulled on my spray skirt, we dragged the bow of the boat into the water and I waded in. John sat on the stern to balance it while I lowered myself into the forward cockpit. Small waves lapped the sides of the boat. John lifted the stern and carried the boat further into the water. Then he stepped in and shoved us off.

After we snapped the elastic-edged spray skirts around the rims of the cockpits, we set out from the tip of the Spit. John was a stronger paddler than I; but from the stern, he matched my pace. Wind blew gently from the southwest, into the mouth of the bay. I focused on paddling. Right, left. Right, left. It wouldn't take that long, I reminded myself. In a little over an hour, we'd be at the south shore.

As we paddled from the tip of the Spit, a few charter boats crossed in front of us on their way back to the harbor. Passengers standing at the sterns in baseball caps and windbreakers stared and waved at us while two-foot-high wakes fanned out from the backs of their boats. John angled our bow into the wakes and when one hit, we rose up and over it, then we prepared for the next.

Once through the traffic, I was relieved. The first hurdle jumped over. Now, to keep going. To cover distance. But also, to look around. The far side of the bay fell into view like layers of a stage set. Offshore rocks: the first painted flat. Then the coastline. Further back, a blue haze washed over each peak with successively more strokes. Then the final blue backdrop of sky. We paddled through a line of driftwood and debris gathered together by the currents. A snarl of bull kelp, its stems knotted by the constant motion of the water, passed off our starboard side. A glaucous-winged gull stood atop a piece of driftwood that bobbed up and down with the surf. We paddled toward a flotilla of half a dozen dainty red-necked phalaropes, the only shorebird that swam in the bay. They spun around themselves in the water like windup bath toys in an effort to suction food from below. In an instant, the birds lifted from the water and flew off in unison. A sea otter popped its head up to catch a glance at us, then lost interest and swam off. Out on the bay, you could see these things: the curiosity of otters, the leisure of gulls. You could witness how birds lived, how the bay slowly gyred, and how the sea was a seamstress and kelp its thread.

Paddling a kayak was the best way to see these things. Unlike being a passenger on a motorized skiff, kayaking was nearly silent, and there was nothing between you and the sea but half a foot of hull. We didn't leak engine oil in watery rainbows behind us, and we could easily pull up onto the narrowest of beaches.

For years, John had explored the watery edges of

lakes and rivers, the coasts of bays and rims of islands. I was learning to do the same. The margin where the sea met the shore was much more interesting than the flat plane of water, and it told you so much about a place. The shore revealed whether the tide was rising or falling and whether the next high tide would be higher or lower than the last. The shore was both a gateway to the land and a piece of the sea floor exposed for view. It displayed the refuse chucked out by the sea: the conical shells of limpets, the snail shells of periwinkles, driftwood licked clean by the surf. We lifted rocks to find crabs, marine worms, eel-like gobi fish, and hopping amphipods. We picked up spiny purple urchins and tossed stranded jelly-fish back into the water. We weeded through tidal wracks and studied stones.

And the edges were never the same. An average of twenty feet of water washed into the bay twice daily with the tide, so a cove could be a wide expanse of water at one point in the day and then a narrow channel girded by mussel flats and tidepools six hours later. The water could rush out like a river, and later sit flat and calm.

When we paddled in the shallows, I could see the bottom. Most of the south shore of the bay had a ragged, rocky coast, and the sea came in clear and free of sediment to the land, rather than cloudy as it did on our side of the bay, which was edged by silty mudflats. Ribbon-like fronds of kelp parted to reveal clams, mussels, and hubcap-sized sea stars of all colors. Moon jellies, a species of jellyfish, pulsed their creamy white tentacles through the bay. Flounders lifted off the bottom and swam away as we approached.

Already that summer, we had fished and collected mussels from our kayaks. A few weeks before, we had paddled across the bay with long-handled landing nets lashed to the deck of the double kayak. We waded into a rushing creek at the head of a narrow inlet that fingered off the bay and caught a dozen red salmon, surging up-stream. Then we cleaned them, lowered them whole into the hatches, and paddled back, exhausted.

There was so much about the region's natural history that I didn't know and couldn't see. I wanted to be able to distinguish between a marbled and a Kittlitz's murrelet, dainty birds that floated on the sea on summer days and flew back to their inland nests in the evenings. I wanted to know the difference between pelagic and red-faced cormorants; both species of these large, black seabirds had the same profile and held their wings open like damp raincoats while they perched on rocks to dry off. But I had begun to notice the differences between the types of sea-weed that collected at the water's edge: which ones were lacy, and which were smooth; which had small, turgid air bladders to keep them afloat and which washed in as flaccid as steamed spinach; which were red, mustard, or green; which felt like waterlogged leather between your fingers and which were as delicate as silk. I was learn-ing things about the water—how a retreating tide left a wet lip on the beach; how glacial streams ran milky into the bay. The previous spring I had taken field trips with my students and had seen some of the bay's microscopic universe: copepods, which looked like helmeted aliens; crab larvae that were large-eyed and leggy; and the larvae of barnacles, which looked like miniature Frisbees with feathery wings.

I had to learn the sea itself, how to navigate it, what to look out for. I was surrounded by capable people and inspired by tough and skillful women. There were women who ran skiffs and who led paddling trips. Others who fished commercially far out in western Alaska while raising children. Some gave birth in remote fish camps, picking nets until labor had undeniably set in. One woman paddled with her husband out of the bay and around the tip of the peninsula on which we lived into the unprotected waters of the Gulf of Alaska. Waves battered this far coastline, and there were stretches of land where rocky cliffs rose straight out of the water, leaving few opportunities to pull ashore.

THE DOUBLE KAYAK was lazy in the water, only inching forward, it seemed, with each stroke. Though more stable, this heavy shell of dinged-up fiberglass was neither agile nor graceful. It was a butter knife compared to the sleek blade of my wooden kayak. Paddling my own boat felt perfect. It was like being on the water in an extension of myself. I would sit with my legs outstretched, the tips of my boots nearly touching the underside of the deck. In my own kayak, if I bent my knees up, I could feel the hull close around me. This tightness made for better maneuverability. The boat would slice neatly through the water and, though it had no rudder, I could turn it easily. With each stroke of my paddle, the nose of my kayak would respond—turning port when I paddled on the right, starboard when I paddled on the left. Gentle rocking of my hips would tip the boat on its keel. The wooden deck would gleam under the sun.

In the double, John leaned on his paddle—dragging it in the water or sweeping the blade around—to turn us. The bow would swing either way, depending on what he did in the stern. My only job was to help keep us going forward, to keep paddling and not stop.

As I turned my head around to see how far we had come, I was glad to have John behind me. "Not too much farther now," he smiled. We were getting to the halfway mark, the no-turning-back point where, even on the calmest of days, the shore seemed much too far away. Behind us, the charter boats had shrunk in the distance and were indistinguishable from each other. Business continued at the tip of the Spit; I felt worlds away. We had told Cynthia we were paddling across for the night, but no one knew we were out there at that moment. No one was watching out for us. No one would know for a long time if anything happened to us.


EARLIER THAT SUMMER, John had gone out paddling alone. He left in the morning with water and lunch and a plan to paddle across the bay and a few miles up it to a cluster of houses, lodges, and oyster farms called Halibut Cove. He said he'd be gone all day, but by nine that night he hadn't returned. It was still light out, but I was worried. I walked out to the edge of the bluff and scanned the bay through binoculars. What if he'd gotten stranded? What if he'd capsized? I called Cynthia. "The same thing happened with Taro years ago," she told me. "I called the harbormaster. He said that almost everyone comes back by ten, because that's when the wind dies down. He said that if Taro wasn't home by then, to call back." Cynthia's husband had returned as predicted, and it was nearly ten when, using binoculars, I spotted the profile of John and his boat nearing the tip of the Spit.

Still, disasters were always happening. The following spring, a deep-sea trawler went down in cold, rough conditions in the Bering Sea, drowning all fifteen men on board. It was the most deadly fishing accident in the country over the past half-century, and it made everyone shudder. Rescuers found only one body.

Two summers later, a young couple went kayaking on a mild January day from the south shore, where they were caretaking a lodge. Both in their mid-twenties, he was writing a novel and she was teaching herself to paint. Though the day they went out was warm and mild for January, the conditions got rough. Their double kayak flipped and they swam to a rocky island. They fumbled up a gravel beach on numb hands and feet, so exhausted and cold that they couldn't think straight and passed out. They woke, climbed a cliff, fell back, and passed out again. He tried to start a fire but failed. When he woke this time, she was gone. Her body had been taken by the tide. He managed to clamber into a cabin on the island and keep himself alive for three days until a passing boat saw him waving from the shore.

"MURRES!" JOHN CALLED, as a couple of black and white birds sped by overhead with their wings beating furiously. I tried to notice other things besides the chop on the water and the breeze teasing the right side of my face and neck. Ahead, scores of black-legged kittiwakes, dainty gull-like birds, had collected on the surface of the water, likely over a ball of needle fish. Far out the mouth of the bay, the familiar red and green hull of a tanker was moving toward us. It would pick up a pilot before heading up the Inlet to a fertilizer plant.

Just past the halfway point, the wind got stronger, and the water began to roll beneath us. The boat rose on two-foot high lumps of sea that were pressing in from the southwest. With each forward motion of our paddles, the rollers spun us nearly a quarter turn on our keel. The waves didn't break, but white water began to lace their tips. Up and down, up and down. I was terrified. In the trough of a wave, the sea curved up around us. At the top, we lost control and could not move ahead or turn.

"John, it's getting worse."

"Wind's picked up," he observed. "But we should be fine."

"Let's paddle hard!" I shouted, knowing nothing else to do or say. Water slipped erratically around my paddle. The rocky islands, where we could rest on the leeward sides, weren't getting closer fast enough. Forward paddle, spin back. Forward paddle, spin back. I could feel the stress in my wrists as I clenched the paddle tightly and used all of my strength to move ahead. Sweat formed in the small of my back, sticking my shirt to my skin, and dampness collected on my forehead beneath the band of my cap.

Far off our bow, boats plied the bay, and I could see the noses of small skiffs dipping into the water as rolling waves passed beneath them. Seeing how the water was playing with these larger boats made me even more nervous. What else were we but a piece of refuse the sea could toss around as it pleased? The sounds of wind and sea and the whine of far-off boat engines made me feel invisible. All I wanted was to catch a whiff of guano from the seabirds that nested on the rocks. The last time we'd paddled across, we could smell the rank, ammonia odor from a quarter-mile away; it was a sign that we were close to the other side. But the wind was at our backs, and we still had more than a mile to go.

I paddled harder. My muscles clenched with nervousness and exertion. What if we lost control and took a wave broadside? What if we got so tired we couldn't continue? Behind us, a skiff engine crescendoed, and a gray-haired man at the wheel slowed near us. "You okay?" he called out to us. It was unusual for paddlers to be on the water in such choppy conditions and even more unusual for kayakers and skiffs to make contact in the middle of the bay.

"Are you okay to keep going?" John asked, his voice raised over the sounds of engine and wind. More than anything, I wanted to climb aboard the skiff, and put a thick hull and fast engine between me and this rolling sea. I wanted to be on dry land. I wanted to be done with it. I knew that if I told John I was too scared to continue, he would call the man over. But he didn't seem nervous and I didn't want to be the one to make us bail out. The man's concern should have confirmed my fear. Instead, I trusted John's calmness. And if I couldn't force myself to keep going, how could I hope to chip away at my fear? I wanted to be rescued but I couldn't say so. I needed John to read me as carefully as he set about reading the sea.

"Sure, let's keep going." The wind blew the words off as soon as they left my mouth.

"We're okay," John shouted back to the man in the skiff.

The boat sped off. We were alone again. The noise of the skiff's idling engine had been a comfort; now it was gone. I paddled as hard as I could and with each stroke felt the weight of the water against the blade. Damp all over from sweat and salt water splashing against our hull, I stared straight ahead at the closest point of land. Mindlessly, I began counting my strokes. One, two, three, four. It kept me focused. I didn't know what John's pace was in the stern and I didn't care. We were moving in too many directions at once: forward then pulled back, buoyed up and then dropped, spun right then pushed left. I squinted at the land ahead and gauged our progress against points on shore. Slowly the south shore of the bay came into focus.

The crossing took us nearly twice as long as it would have in flat water. By the time we reached the other side, we'd given up plans to paddle up a fjord to a campsite we'd located on the map. Instead, we headed over to a nearby gravel beach and got out of the boat. We lifted the bow onto the beach so that the kayak wouldn't drift away. We exchanged few words as we opened the hatches and unpacked, carrying the gear up above the high tide line. The tide would peak around midnight, and we needed to make sure that everything was safely stowed. Then we carried the boat—John at the stern, me at the bow—into grass above the high-tide line. We would pitch a tent next to it for the night.

"I hated that," was all I could say as I slumped onto the cobbles, feeling the tension in my body beginning to let go for the first time since we'd landed. "Yeah, that wasn't much fun," John agreed. I was relieved that he had been uncomfortable too, but I wanted to scream, *why did we do this? Couldn't you see I was terrified?* But I didn't. John sat down next to me and put his arm around my shoulders. As waves drained down the beach, they raked the cobbles against each other, making a loud but calming sound. We were finally on land. In two days, we would have to make the crossing again, heading home. My stomach would be uneasy until we were back on the other side of the bay.

The weight of John's arm—it wasn't enough to comfort me. It never would be. I needed to learn to trust my own fear, to let myself be terrified. I needed to remember that fear helps keep people alive. I thought of my beautiful kayak back home. Would the way it held me so carefully, so specifically, give me the confidence I lacked? Or would it gather dust? There weren't many weeks left of summer to figure it out. It would take a year before the answers to those questions became clear, but much longer to realize that it was too easy to pick up a man's dream, his measure of the world, rather than fashion one of my own.

# 7

# FALL

VIGIA: *n. A rock or shoal the position of which is doubtful, or a warning note to this effect on the chart.*

Fall brought a vibrant explosion of decay. The leaves burst into color before dropping, and grasses in the tidal slough in the middle of town flashed gold and then went drab. Roadsides grabbed colors, it seemed, out of the air—holding red, yellow, green, and brown all at once, while the blue and orange of the few late lupine and daisies that hung on intensified as everything else senesced around them. Birches boldly appeared in yellow where they'd been blending in green all summer long among spruce, and the alpine slopes across the bay came into startling focus during those last moments before snow.

Most people thought of fall as the end of the season; for me, it was a beginning. Since moving to Alaska in the fall two years before, that season had felt like the beginning of it all, of my life here, of the cycle of a year. Fall reminded me why I'd come here—to see what it was to live at the edge of wilderness. I had wanted to see how the life I imagined I might live here would simplify my needs. But instead of paring down my desires, being here expanded them. I needed a freezer full of wild salmon and berries. I needed undeveloped coastline. I needed silence and untracked snow. I needed the abrupt swings between seasons to wake me up. I needed to see owls. Having been raised to think I could do anything, be anybody, I never thought about compromise. There was danger in that.

FALL DIDN'T PASS here lazily as it did where I grew up. There were no weeks of falling leaves, no weekends spent raking them into jumping-into piles. There was no dank earth smell out the back door or strings of evenings when crows would gather in one of the few remaining stands of tulip poplars and shout at rush hour traffic. Here fall was a moment. John and I were eager to experience it before winter settled in. On a Sunday in mid-September, we got in the car and headed east from our house. We were driving "out east," as people called it, which meant taking the road that ran eastward from the blinking red light along the north shore of the bay toward its head. This wasn't to be confused with "*back* East," which referred to the East Coast. We passed grassy fields interspersed with houses and clumps of alders and spruce. We passed an old bus with a stovepipe stuck out of the roof. I had heard that one of my students lived in there. We passed a low building just off the road that was a bar and package store, a church housed in a double-wide trailer, and another church that was a two-story geodesic dome made out of plywood painted yellow. We passed a greenhouse that had been fashioned out of two-by-fours and plastic sheeting. The couple who lived in the house next to it—a plywood, box-shaped structure—were growing English cucumbers to sell in town. The greenhouse had collapsed during the winter under snow, and the owners had rigged it up again in the spring.

We were driving along the bench, which was stippled by a wide range of types of houses—from half-million-dollar second homes with bright blue or green metal roofs and large windows facing the bay to unfinished places with tar paper flapping in the wind, surrounded by generations of old cars and trucks. Local economics were changing as retirees moved in, bringing money they'd made someplace else and leaving behind children who were having kids of their own. This influx of cash changed things: Subdivisions were being stamped out of patches of alder, and tidy houses were thrown up—built on spec—that looked out of place in their neatness and completeness.

Eight miles out of town, the Fritz Creek General Store, a low log structure, offered a two-pump gas station, post office, liquor store, movie rental, fresh bread, pizza, and espresso. In the summer, you could pick a few dusty raspberries at the edge of the gravel parking lot, and in the winter, find underemployed locals socializing inside. Across the street sat the most expensive restaurant around Homer, which served seafood and steaks. During the summer, tourists flocked to the place, which had been written up in all of the guide books.

Past the general store and restaurant, the road gained elevation as it headed through acres of dead but still-standing spruce. Over the previous decade, an infestation of spruce bark beetles, an insect the size of a piece of long grain rice, had killed an area of spruce forest outside of town as large as Connecticut. These beetles crawled under the bark of trees and laid eggs. Hungry larvae emerged and sucked the sap of the tree until the canopy went brown and the tree died. Spruce that had stood dead for three or four years weren't much good for building. There was a push to tidy things up, to get private companies to log the dead trees even on public land in places that would require new roads. "Salvage logging," it was called, and it grew more popular as wildfires raged through the grayed woods. But dead spruce slowly rotting into the ground provided the best nursery for young ones. And when the trees were clear-cut, grass typically choked out everything else.

The beetles had been killing spruce in the region in cycles for hundreds of years. But by the late 1980s, the climate here was warming measurably. The winters got milder and the summers warmer, causing a historic population explosion among the beetles. In less than ten years the forests were leveled. "We were shell-shocked," an old-timer told me. As the woods fell, houses that had been closely hugged by spruce now stood naked, bare to the road and to neighbors. Some homes enjoyed a bay and glacier view for the first time, but these new views raised property taxes. A couple who had homesteaded this forested land forty years earlier couldn't get used to the expansive vista and moved into town.

Twenty-three miles out of town to the east, the pavement ended at the school bus turnaround, a geographical point familiar to everyone in town. The school bus was a civilizing factor; if you lived beyond the turnaround, you were *really* off the map. There, a line of mailboxes sat next to a bullet-pocked sign that warned "ROAD NARROWS." A brown sign tacked up temporarily beneath it by the state's Fish and Game department explained moose hunting regulations. It was the season for moose and ducks. This was fall.

A few miles past the turnaround, the dirt road ended at a small clearing where an old sedan missing a wheel was propped on a wood block, and a rusted horse trailer lay on its side in the grass. At the edge of the clearing, a cemetery opened behind a gate topped by a Russian Orthodox cross with three bars—the third low and slanted down to the right. Beyond the clearing, a steep dirt track switchbacked down to the beach. Near where this road met the beach was a village of Old Believers that was represented by a single black dot on the map. I had never heard of Old Believers before moving to Alaska, but I learned of them quickly after seeing entrance and exit marked in both English and Russian on the doors of the main supermarket. Old Believers, a sect of Russian Orthodox, had broken off from the church in the mid-seventeenth century after the patriarch at the time mandated changes in church books and rituals to correct what he considered inaccuracies and inconsistencies. It has been estimated that tens of thousands of Old Believers burned themselves in protest. Others fled their villages and pledged to fervently uphold a traditional religious life. In small communities, they moved to undeveloped areas of Russia or left to roam the globe in search of places—China, Australia, Brazil—where they could live and raise children away from the influences of modern life.

Mainstream Russian Orthodoxy had come to Alaska when the Russians first arrived and raised churches topped by the characteristic triple-barred crosses on the banks of muddy rivers and on patches of wind-swept tundra. You can find these churches in poor Native villages all over the state; their cheap chandeliered and fake-gilded interiors are the most opulent things around. But Old Believer communities, where Russian was spoken even in public schools, came later: They migrated from Oregon in the mid-1960s and formed about half a dozen villages in Southcentral Alaska, four of which were within twenty-five miles of Homer.

John parked the car next to the overturned horse trailer and we got out. The clearing was close to the edge of the bluff, and beyond its edge, the sun shone on the head of the bay, turning it turquoise. Shadows of clouds moved like dark islands over the water. Fireweed, long past its fuchsia bloom, draped the bluff with scarlet leaves down to the beach. Although the flowers were done, the blaze of the plant was even fiercer at this time of year. Across the bay, Dixon Glacier glowed pale blue between treeless slopes that were losing their lush green.

There was a kind of panic in the air at this time of year. The light rapidly dwindled, and you knew that snow, which would begin falling at any time, threatened to hide everything uncovered for the next seven months. You sealed cracks, brought in lawn equipment, and set your mind to withstand the dark and cold. Winterizing was a process of getting your affairs in order. I never seemed to have things figured out. The days were perpetually falling out from beneath me; my feeling of unpreparedness swelled.

ON FOOT, WE headed down the steep dirt road that switchbacked to the beach. This road was the easiest way down to the head of the bay and the only route to the Old Believer village. But we'd heard that the road belonged to the village, and that only "the Russians," which is how people referred to them, were allowed to drive it. The track was narrow and steeply pitched, with vertical walls cut into the bluff along it. As we descended, I pictured the road during spring breakup, when frost heaves would crack its surface and leave deep ruts and dangerously soft spots.

By most standards, we were in a remote place—more than twenty miles to the nearest hospital, half a dozen off pavement, far from city water and sewer lines. As you traveled out east, the houses got less frequent, in many cases more rustic. There were dozens of rental cabins out here without running water and parcels of land on which young couples were clearing to build. You could see black and brown bears out here, moose, wolves, and lynx; you never heard a siren, and couldn't count on fire crews if your house caught on fire.

The sound of an engine approached, and a late-model white Jeep passed us on its way up the switchback. A Russian woman sat alone at the wheel as the car bucked up the rutted track. She wore the characteristic head scarf, which we'd seen on Old Believer women who came into town to shop and do errands. In town, their traditional dress set them apart from the rest of us. The women wore ankle-length, pastel dresses and kept their hair in two long braids tied up in a fabric that matched their dresses. The men wore high-neck, embroidered shirts and grew beards. The children dressed like miniature adults. Although the Old Believers kept to themselves, everyone in town had something to say about them and it was usually not good. "They drink too much and throw beer cans out the windows of their trucks." "They skip out on taxes by buying their cars through their church." "They abuse their women and work their girls too hard." A few minutes later, two trucks passed us—driven by Russian men—and then two four-wheelers roared by, loaded with two Russian boys apiece. The remoteness of the head of the bay, we realized, didn't mean peace and quiet.

After about a mile, the road flattened into a track along the beach. It was nearly high tide, and the mudflats had been overtaken by a shallow layer of cloudy water that pressed mussel shells, eelgrass, and driftwood toward the shore. John stopped, raised his binoculars, and looked out over the bay. "Snow geese," he said. "About two hundred of them. They must be gathering before going south." I lifted my binoculars and saw grains of gleaming white way off in the distance. I wouldn't have known what they were, but as soon as he said it, I saw that they could be nothing else.

Just off the beach sat a slanted but well-kept log cabin on a fenced patch of grass. A dozen cows grazed in the yard. The cabin belonged to the oldest of eight children of a Swiss family who staked out property near Homer in the 1930s. The parents had fled the rise of Nazism, and sought to create an agrarian utopia in which to raise a family. It was a life of hard work. Two generations later, the wide face of one of their grandchildren—Jewel, the pop music star—gleamed from the covers of celebrity magazines.

Beyond the cabin and a log bridge that spanned a small creek, the road turned away from the beach into the Russian village. From our vantage point on the beach, the village was a collection of drab-colored houses enclosed by a fence of metal posts and barbed wire. NO TRESPASS-ING signs had been tacked to the trunks of nearby trees. Cows grazing along the edge of the fence lifted their heads as we walked by, but no one else was around. About 250 people lived in the village, which was owned in collective by the community. The school building, too, belonged to the village and was leased to the district, which ran a small school where American teachers, assisted by Russian aides, taught classes of only Russian children. I had never been in the village—the signs were enough to keep me out—but a woman I knew who had taught there for sixteen years told me it was a beautiful place with neat gardens overflowing with vegetables, wood-sided houses, the school, and the church. Every morning, she parked her car at the top of the road and hiked in. For most of the school year, the mornings were dark and she used a headlamp to illuminate the way. At the end of the day, she hiked back out. Often, she had to attach cleats to her boots for traction on the steep road. She loved teaching there, she told us. She felt accepted and appreciated by the community. Russian kids typically didn't attend school past their mid-teen years; none from the village had made it through high school. Boys took off to begin careers as commercial fishermen, while girls, once married, became responsible for a growing household. In her late-forties, my friend was already teaching the children of some of her first students.

Although many of the Old Believers had been born here, they spoke Russian at home and maintained a distinct separateness from town life. We never saw them at restaurants or community celebrations; they didn't go to the movie theater or local bars. The children learned English in school, yet it might be years for them between trips into town. It was a village life, and the role of mayor passed among the men year to year. I wondered about the Russian women my own age: toting around huge families

while wearing high-waisted dresses—maternity clothing year in and year out—they seemed ultrafeminine, yet
must have been indomitably tough.

Aside from the old cabin, the village, and one house
beyond the village with a fenced horse pasture, there was
no other development around. There was no pavement,
no streetlights, no stores or restaurants. The only way out
was back up the dirt switchback.

We walked along the barbed wire toward the head
of the bay. This was one of the most remote parts of the
bay, but the beach here was ugly and felt industrial. There
was no sand, just mudflats and above them, the land was
chipped up coal and red baked shale—which looked like
crumbled clay pots, ground finer under the tire tracks.
The mudflats were littered with the dribbled castings of
marine worms, and a jellyfish puddled on the mud, looking like a pool of oil. There was trash: large truck tires,
a box that once held rifle cartridges, beer bottles, and
fleshless scapula that likely were butchering waste from
a moose carcass. Figure eights had been tracked into the
mudflats by four-wheelers. Algae grew filmy in depressions that once held water, and driftwood stained orange
by iron in the mud lay piled like a stack of defunct ma-
chine parts. Just over the fence, fifty-five-gallon drums
lay half-buried in the mud, and a heap of rubble marked
where a building had once stood—snarled metal sheets,
torn yellow insulation, cut wires, two-by-fours stuck
with nails—and an empty boat form sat beneath a plywood shed that was collapsing around it.

I found it surprising that this community, which seemed to pay such careful attention to how its members lived, would have let the beach get trashed. I had a romantic notion of the Old Believer life—of an idyllic existence of fishing, gardening, and God—unspoiled by the desires and refuse that cluttered the modern lives of the rest of us. But the communities of Old Believers were a confounding mix of the old and the new. There were few concrete rules, but the Russians shunned modern technology, even computers in the schools. Men didn't shave their beards, and they kept strict fasts around the holidays. Even their language was old. "That is the Russian we speak," a Russian aide had told the teacher I knew, pointing to a children's book written by Tolstoy before the turn of the last century. It was village Russian, a language that encompassed an older, rural life. Yet the men drove new trucks and the women could be seen wheeling around town in shiny sedans and SUVs. I would often see the mothers in the main supermarket in town, wearing their handmade dresses and surrounded by a clutch of children. I'd notice cases of Diet Pepsi, packages of hot dogs, and other modern treats filling their carts.

The Old Believers weren't the only Alaskans who cobbled together a life that was a mixture of old and new, modern and traditional. Everywhere I looked, I saw the homestead mentality of self-reliance and resourcefulness contrasting with dependence on modern conveniences. You could find young couples living out of town in dark cabins without running water who took two-week winter vacations in Hawaii. There were houses heated by woodstoves that had gleaming white satellite dishes standing next to them. Though I was fiercely committed to harvesting wild food whenever I could, my life was modern: I drove into town to work and came home to a warm house that had running water, a television, my CD collection. John and I put up salmon but we also bought imported goat cheese. About two-thirds of the state's population lived in cities, but these "cities" were minutes away from vast tracts of wilderness. Alaska was ranked highest in the country for Internet access, while over the course of a year Alaskans harvested eighty pounds of wild food per capita. Certainly not everyone hunted, fished, or gathered, but the fall issues of the *Anchorage Daily News*, the state's largest newspaper, showed that these traditional activities were on many people's minds; articles discussed duck hunting etiquette, caribou quotas, tips for sizing antlers accurately, alpine ptarmigan hunting, and a successful suburban moose hunt.

Nowhere was this combination of modern and traditional lifestyles as profound as with Alaska Natives. Their ancestors had been here for thousands of years, and contemporary Natives held on to many of the old ways while picking up many of the new. They used outboards on whale hunts and to bring families to fish camps where they would stay for weeks to net and dry fish to eat throughout the rest of the year. They drove snowmachines for hunting, transportation, and entertainment, and to collect driftwood for traditional sweat baths. They traveled to small villages off the road system by plane. And, like everyone else in the state, they relied on cars and trucks, and on the delivery of groceries and mail by road, sea, or air. Assimilation like this was nothing new. Since the white man first arrived in Alaska, the Native peoples to varying degrees had picked up their dress, their church, their diseases, and their liquor.

The drilling of the first commercially viable oil well pushed Alaska into statehood in 1959. And ten years later, when ten billion barrels of oil were discovered at Prudhoe Bay in the Alaskan Arctic, legislators rushed to parcel out a land area nearly one-fifth the size of the Lower 48 so that jurisdiction could be determined and a pipeline could be built across the state to get this oil to market. Officials pledged to allow Alaska Natives to retain control over their villages and the land that they used for hunting, fishing, and gathering food. The white man could think of no other way to arrange this control except by organizing tribes into for-profit corporations. This system made sense to people who had been using paper money for centuries. In 1971, through the Alaska Native Claims Settlement Act, in exchange for giving up aboriginal land claims by Alaska Natives—claims to almost all of the state's land—the federal government gave title to one-ninth of the state's land area and all the resources they contained to these new Native-owned corporations. Overnight, Native people became shareholders. In order to turn a profit for their shareholders, the corporations, which were organized by region, would have to sell or develop their land. No longer could the landscape merely provide fresh meat, fish, berries, clams, and wood—it could help you buy a truck. With land now a resource in a cash economy, the tensions between traditions and the corporate bottom line grew fierce. Hard lines of ownership and jurisdiction suddenly appeared. And a way of life built—out of necessity—on self-reliance was whittled away when do-gooder federal agencies doled out housing and food. Welfare undermined the skill and stamina required to provide these things for one's family, and chipped away at self-worth. Diabetes rates in villages skyrocketed as diets were "modernized" toward mass-produced consumer foods. Urban fashions such as low-slung jeans and cocked baseball caps crept into these communities, while the traditional dress made out of gut, skins, and fur could be found more often behind glass. Over time the Native corporations got savvy. These days some of them were pulling in billions of dollars' worth of preferential minority contracts with the Defense Department and other federal entities for construction, maintenance, and security. But as consumer culture trampled traditional cultures, and a lack of skills, education, and connections shut many Alaska Natives out of the modern definition of success, alcohol and drug use soared. "Suicide" became a verb.

Alaska was changing rapidly. We could see it every day: Undeveloped parcels were razed and built upon, roads were widened and paved, new tracks were being punched through spruce woods, and new businesses were bringing in the kind of luxuries we had complained you couldn't get here—coconut milk, foreign films, fashionable clothes. In Anchorage, the airport was being renovated from a dingy yet practical structure to one of those gleaming shopping mall–like complexes so common in the Lower 48. The city's demographics were diversifying to match those of big cities elsewhere in the country, and gang violence—a modern echo of frontier vigilantism—was rearing its head. But in Alaska, you still could have that feeling of going someplace undeveloped, of standing on a patch of ancient earth where no one else had been before. This is what makes the frontier so deliciously new and inviting. We were surrounded by wilderness, by landscapes uncluttered by modern facades. Here you could see ancient history around you: primeval ice grinding out valleys across the bay, million-year-old imprints of leaves, seams of coal that recalled a completely different climate. Here you could see entire watersheds, and, if you looked closely, you could see the histories of those watersheds: old beaver ponds grown over with willows; rivers that inched sideways; lakes that were sneaking across valleys, carrying their far shore with them and leaving a trail of new green growth.

WE TOOK OFF our boots and socks and rolled up our jeans to cross a swift creek that ran cold and cloudy above knee-deep. On the other side, I sat on a log in the sun to dry off and put my gear back on. John stood barefoot on a large, flat rock scanning with his binoculars. The trail curved around a thick stand of alders and there, the steep bluffs that lined the north shore of the bay pushed back, opening vast flats in front of us. Short marsh plants painted the mudflats yellow-green. This area was the bay's nursery, refuge, and pantry. Streams dropped inland nutrients to feed a wide network of marshes, cut by river channels; here shorebirds fattened up, seals pupped in large groups, moose dropped calves, bears scavenged, and ducks dabbled all winter long.

John trailed his binoculars after a black speck moving across the sky. "Falcon," he pronounced. "Probably a peregrine." He'd noticed the bird's speed, pointed wings, and short tail. By the time I stood up and raised my binoculars to my eyes, it was gone. He wanted to see and name the birds to make sense out of where he was. He needed to know what was there to feel at ease in a place, and to feel as though he'd truly experienced his own life. Not looking and not knowing would be a missed opportunity, a life less full. But when we spotted a bird together, I'd often shout, "Don't say! Don't say!" ordering him not to identify it aloud. I wanted to name it for myself. I wanted to know whether I was making progress. Was I seeing the difference between a dunlin and dowitcher at a distance? Could I tell a mallard from a shoveler at a glance? I memorized names and field marks.

A shot sounded in the distance, then echoed. Far out on the flats, ducks rose into the air like fruit unfalling from a tree. I scanned around with my binoculars and made out a couple of duck hunters on a four-wheeler far out on the flats. A yellow dog bounded ahead of them. At the end of the day the hunters would head home with the supple, streamlined bodies of freshly shot ducks lashed to the back of their four-wheeler. The feathers would bare colors few people saw: the shimmering hues of blue, green, and purple that birds revealed only on close examination.

It was late afternoon and we hadn't gotten to any landmarks. There was no sign announcing the head of the bay. Nothing that said this is how far you've come, how far you have left to go. I had hoped a trip to the head of the bay would reveal the answer to a question I couldn't yet form.

We turned back under a canopy of cottonwoods. In late spring, the trees had shaken out their white cotton flakes. This hint of winter wasn't subtle. Summer sped by and fall, we knew, would pass in a blink. Back on the beach, the tide had gone out, exposing a million tiny drainages that had carved shallow rivulets in the mud. Chunks of coal and knots of red kelp had been abandoned when the bay pulled back. Nearly half a dozen tidal wracks ran along the beach—empty mussel shells, seaweed that had dried into fists, vacant crabs, the donut-shaped skeletons of urchins—cleaned, spineless, and bleached white. We collected a few clumps of mussels that had washed up with the tide. Their byssal threads, strong hairlike strands that anchored them to rocks and each other, had trapped small stones and empty mussel shells. We ripped off the large mussels and threw everything else back onto the mudflats. This would be dinner.

Here it seemed we could do it all—collect mussels on the beach for dinner, rent a new release at the video store to watch afterward. Maybe it was perfect. Maybe it was jarring. Sometimes it seemed it couldn't last. Sometimes I imagined life in the Bush, off the road system, surviving primarily off the land. I felt I needed to prove myself like that—to no one else but me.

"Alaska's the only place where a man can be a man," a rough-around-the-edges bachelor told me. He carried a sharp knife on his belt and lived without running water, with an outhouse and woodstove. Most days he split wood. For much of the year, he had to walk or ski three quarters of a mile to his house. He worked in town as an electrician only as much as he had to. Lately, the bachelor had taken to wintering in the tropics.

Women here were just as likely as men to seek a physical, demanding life. And they seemed, generally, more adept than men at straddling two worlds—at holding down regular, even professional, positions in town while tending the garden, putting up fish, keeping a modern homestead going. Perhaps they were better at knowing what they needed and seeking it out. We worked and played; we needed the most intimate of relations and to be alone, to get away. Women formed their own social networks: book clubs, dance groups, knitting circles, art collectives, gardening associations. But, as I could see from many women around me—between job and home, harvest and play, meetings and solitude—the search for the simple life could be incredibly complex.

This mixed life embodied so many paradoxes. To live off the land requires supplies brought in from someplace else. It requires machines that you have to keep feeding with gas and oil. It requires access by highway, plane, or boat. Remoteness is often at the cost of long phone calls to friends and family elsewhere. I traveled more miles by plane those first years in Alaska than I'd done in the whole of my life up to that point. When I went back to the East Coast to visit my family, I was always surprised at the newness of things: late model cars gleaming across freshly paved roads painted with crisp lines; neatly trimmed lawns buttoned up around houses like pressed shirts; people wearing fresh haircuts and new clothes. The glimmer attracted and repelled me. Sometimes I got sick of wearing old jeans and rubber boots. I would buy a strappy sundress at the mall and take it back to Alaska where I'd fold it and put it away in the bottom of my drawer. I wanted to be handy, and I wanted to be beautiful.

As JOHN AND I walked along the beach, I thought about the future of the Old Believers. In a few years, a pair of teens would graduate from high school in this village, pulling other students behind them in the years after. Already a few young women from other Russian villages were attending the community college in town. More would soon follow. Would the village suddenly pick up and move to some untrammeled patch of land in Canada or Argentina or who knows where else in an effort to stay intact? Would they have to choose between maintaining their traditions and holding onto their geography?

Sometimes living here, I felt I had to choose between the wonders of nature and the wonders of human ingenuity. On the East Coast, every old city block was a reminder of human potential: prewar apartment buildings with intricate facades, highly engineered parks, old churches. Concerts, galleries, and museums exhibited extraordinary talent while here, most talent was homegrown. In Alaska, the beauty of the land and sea was unparalleled and the extent of undeveloped terrain was greater than anywhere else in the United States. But sometimes for me, this wasn't enough. I wanted to lead both lives.

John seemed sure he wanted this life, wanted to buy, build, stay, while for me it was more complicated than that. The future came into focus in his mind with perfect over-the-shoulder light. For me, it was a fuzzy thing in the distance, as when I forgot my binoculars or rain blurred the view of the mountains across the bay. "Are you going to stay? Are you thinking about buying a place?" I was asked one day at the bookstore by a woman I barely knew. Her questions drilled too deep into me. People here talked about foundations, frames, and property lines. I couldn't grasp this language of permanence. Even so, more than anything, I wanted to feel at home here—at home catching and putting up fish, running a skiff, knowing whom everyone was referring to when they mentioned names around town, knowing the bird calls when they sounded new once again in the spring. Yet sometimes the landscape here repulsed me. The stunted spruce seemed sickly and pathetic. The few deciduous trees were short and scrawny, the array of spring warblers dull. The bars too smoky, the Friday nights too quiet.

"You're having a great experience," friends back East would say. I wanted to explain that this was just life, that it wasn't hard enough or extreme enough, that I hadn't proved anything to myself about how I could live or whether I could take care of myself. That I hadn't let go of my lust for fancy shoes, I had just lost the opportunity to wear them in this life dominated by gravel, snow, and mud.

Somewhere among all of our dreams and disappointments, we have to piece together a compromise. Nothing is clear-cut—not how we live, not our desires, not one love affair from its predecessor, not the differences between the life we lead and another we could make for ourselves somewhere else. If you really looked at anything—the Russian village, life in Native villages, the lives adopted here by those of us who had come from far away—you would see a confounding amalgam. But compromise wasn't yet part of my language. Wanting so many different things left me with a quiet, constant ache.

AFTER TURNING BACK, we spotted two Russian girls, about nine years old, on the beach up ahead. They were dragging pieces of driftwood twice their height up the beach as the wind tousled their long, white dresses. Their braids swung across their backs as they lunged with the wood, trying to balance the tops of the trunks against each other, making a tepee. "Hurry up!" one of the girls called to the other. "Get that one under!" The English surprised me. The other girl responded in Russian as they fitted the ends against each other. Then the construction began as they balanced more sections of driftwood, closing the walls of the wood tent. They laughed as they worked, and then stopped to watch us as we walked by. We waved and they waved back.

In a few weeks, rain would extinguish the colorful burn of fall. Birch and cottonwood canopies would fizzle out like embers. After the season of bounty, life would pare way down. The grasses would die back; the trees would undress. The bay would scour the beach clean and snow would simplify everything: hummocks flattened to a white plane, gnarled mountain slopes made smooth. The landscape would become a husk of its former self as the night sky hunched up behind the daytime dome. But the tide would always bring gifts. We would eat well.

# 8

## WINTER

NILAS: *n. A thin elastic crust of ice, easily bending on waves and swell and under pressure, thrusting in a pattern of interlocking fingers.*

M y second winter was different. Friends and family back East kept asking me when I was coming home. Home? When would they realize that my real life had begun and that I *was* home? . . . Wasn't I?

On a Sunday morning in early March, when the sky was white and changeless, the light dull and without angle, John and I put on our skis, which we stored tips-up in the waist-high mound of snow outside the front door, and headed downhill into a shallow creek drainage. The previous fall, we had moved into a house in the hills behind town at the end of a one-mile gravel road walled by spruce. We watched the snow pile up outside our windows and ice send lace up the glass, until we could no longer remember what the yard looked like when not covered by four feet of clean cotton batting.

On weekend days, we'd pack water, cookies, and a

thermos of hot soup and ski until dark. We could ski for miles out the front door of the house, dipping into valleys and skiing along the humped backs of hills. We skirted clumps of alder, fallen spruce, and willow thickets that stuck through the snow. We passed abandoned home-steaders' cabins and carefully furnished summer cabins surrounded by snow untouched by truck, plow, or shovel; we could press our noses up to the windows knowing that the owners weren't likely to return until June.

The few inches of new snow that had fallen the night before sat atop an icy crust that held our weight in the coldness of the morning. I pushed off ahead of John, past the browned elderberry shrub which splayed up through the snow like the bottom of an old broom. I moved with a skater's stride, trying to build momentum to carry me down the hill. I glided my right ski out and then the left. I pushed the ground behind me with my poles, feeling them pierce the hard crust beneath the powder.

The sky's white ceiling felt close and heavy above us as we skied along the edge of the driveway. It wouldn't snow or rain all day. We kept our skis just at the edge of the road; it was a steep drop down to the track. A plow no longer could do the job of keeping the driveway open, so a huge snowblower truck had sucked a channel through the snow, leaving straight snow walls halfway up the windows of our cars. I had just bought my first car, a red, ten-year-old station wagon with four-wheel drive. Now I had my own vehicle to take care of, which meant I had to put on studded tires each fall, change the oil regularly, and watch out for rust spreading along the wheel wells.

It had been a mild winter to start. It rained for weeks, throwing dead spruce into creeks where they clogged culverts and flooded streets. But by February, snow pushed out the rain and layered deeply outside of town. John and I continued to teach at the small schools where we had been hired the year before. In the morning, we left our place in the dark. By nine, the growing dawn silhouetted the mountain range across the bay, though the sky would still be strung with stars. In midwinter, it wouldn't be light until half past ten. It would be dark by the time we came home. On days when we returned to our place to find snow too deep on the part of our road the borough didn't plow, we parked our cars in a narrow pullout half a mile from the house and skied home. In the morning, we skied back to the cars wearing headlamps over wool hats. We stashed our skis in the backs of our cars and drove to work. The city and borough maintained armies of plow trucks so that school was never closed because of snow, but occasionally, freezing rain or high winds canceled school. Because the beetle epidemic had killed so many of the spruce trees around town, strong winds coupled with root-loosening downpours often prompted officials to close the schools: Dead trees threatened to fall onto power lines, across roads, and onto school roofs and buses.

The director of the school where I taught was a stout, practical woman who had nearly shoulder-length gray hair and wore boys' sneakers. She missed her sons, who were off at college, but was relieved that her husband had moved away. A string of troubled teenagers moved through her place, which was a collection of buildings without running water in various stages of being built or remodeled about a dozen miles outside of town—a brother and sister whose abused mother walked through town trying to avoid talking to people; a teenage girl from somewhere else who had somehow landed on the school's doorstep; and a young woman who had lived there for so long that she helped bring the others up to speed: huskies to be fed outside, Chihuahuas and cats indoors.

I was so busy worrying about the fact that many of the kids would never master algebra that for a while I failed to grasp the real point: The director just wanted to get them through school so that they could find jobs, become independent, and move on with their lives. Moving on—and sometimes leaving town—was exactly what they needed to do. But I earnestly stuck to my failed vision. On Monday mornings I posted a riddle on the wall for the students to solve by the end of the week; Friday mornings, I ran science demonstrations. But the kids preferred to socialize rather than solve the riddles, and the science demonstrations usually flopped. And on the day when I looked out the window in the middle of teaching a biology lesson and saw cars swaying in their parking spaces, shaken by tremors deep in the Earth, I was the only one who wanted to run outside. The kids just looked up from their work and laughed.

IN THE WINTER, as shore ice clutches Alaska's northern coast like a blanket pulled up under the chin, wind scours the state's Arctic plain, endlessly drifting and sculpting its light snowfalls. In the Interior, snow piles up—each winter an average of five and a half feet drops on Fairbanks—and the temperature of the still air in this region dives deeply below zero. Far to the southwest, out in the Aleutian Islands, winter storms bring endless snow, rain, and wind. In the Southcentral part of the state, low pressure fronts spin off the Gulf of Alaska, sucking bitter air down from the north, bringing moist air inland, and dropping snow. Along the coast here, winter dumps foot after foot of snow—in the fishing town of Cordova, nestled in Prince William Sound, an average of seven feet falls each winter. As you go south toward Alaska's Panhandle, snow more often turns to rain.

Winter's coldest weather seemed irrational. When it came, dry slush—like some sort of lunar dust—formed on the beach at the edge of the surf. On cold, clear nights under a gibbous moon, ice crystals sparkled fantastically across the surface of the snow, as though it were illuminated from within. Cloudless nights often draped otherworldly colors across the sky—neon green, fuchsia, ghostly white—as though the aurora borealis were dropping silk handkerchiefs to Earth. Sometimes the northern lights just glowed on the horizon like a second moon readying to rise. Cold fronts occasionally slid into town and didn't budge, depositing a gray ice fog that trapped wood smoke and car exhaust until the air around town smelled like the end of a tailpipe. In the hills behind town, frigid air sank into the creek drainages, lacquering willows with ice. In bitter weather, supple fabric became stiff and noisy, and even the snow squeaked. Our eyelashes and hair grayed when moisture from our exhalations froze onto the strands. Car doors iced shut, engines grumbled to a start more grumpily than normal—or didn't start at all—and ice spread along the insides of windshields. The coldest days were too cold for snow and brought a dry air devoid of smells that scraped my throat.

The darkness and the cold, the raging wind and persevering snowstorms, and the incessant, frigid crash of the sea would seem to shut Alaskans in their homes during the long winter. But the time of snow and ice is the time when much of Alaska is its most open. Winter makes the landscape—otherwise soggy, lake-speckled, and river-sliced in so much of the state—far more traversable than during the thawed months. Snow makes the endless rolling land quietly navigable for miles by smoothing rumpled ground, masking tangled shrubs, and bridging creeks. Along Alaska's northern coast, shore ice makes travel between villages more direct as sinuous bays and inlets could be bypassed. Frozen rivers in the north become state-maintained highways that link remote villages. Fuel trucks, family station wagons, and state trooper vehicles travel the curving river highways that are marked with stakes and reflective tape and kept open from the incessantly drifting snow by plow trucks. A fleet of taxis—Chevy Suburbans, mostly—carry villagers into town for supplies, or ferry them to and from their ice fishing spots on the river.

But this mobility often invited disaster. Each winter triggered a relay of deaths. As soon as the old man who sped away from his village into the white expanse on his snowmachine was pronounced gone, a boat would capsize in winter waters. A truck driver was killed when an avalanche spilled him across the highway and into the ocean, and a helicopter dove into cold, gray water. A recluse died of hypothermia when the power company shut off his electricity, and an old woman, suffering from dementia, wandered out of her home to freeze to death alone.

Even small things could spell death in winter: car keys dropped—and lost—in the snow on a frigid night, a stalled-out snowmachine far from help, a minor miscalculation on an icy highway. A single page of the *Anchorage Daily News* reported two days' toll of winter deaths: A boy died when he sledded into a stationary truck; a couple was killed when a young man lost control of his speeding truck on an icy highway; an avalanche tumbled an experienced skier down a mountain and buried him under five feet of snow while his friend watched; and a young man was killed when a downdraft smashed the single-engine plane his father was piloting into a remote, snow-covered valley. The radio, too, droned with disaster all winter long. We kept the statewide news on while we cooked dinner. That winter, there was nearly one death a week from snowmachine accidents alone. Winter united this broad swath of continent. Here, Alaskans all over the state heard of the misfortunes everywhere else. Winter was winter for us all.

And the cold months meant a new set of precautions. You considered backup heat in case the power went out for an extended time. You checked the level of fuel oil in your tank before the snow made the driveway impassable to oil trucks. You made sure the pipes didn't freeze during a sudden cold snap or when you went away. If roofs weren't designed right, they sloughed off snow at the foot of the front door, and you kept a bucket of sand nearby to scatter on icy steps and paths. For long road trips, we often kept a snow shovel in the back of the car, as well as water, a sleeping bag, food, and matches.

Weaving between stands of spruce, we passed the nearest neighboring home, an A-frame cabin that shared our half-mile drive. We often saw our neighbor, a young guy with curly, strawberry blond hair who was trailed by an overweight black lab, splitting wood in front of his place with a hand-rolled cigarette drooping from his lower lip. Derek made his rent by transcribing music sent to him via email by composers in the Lower 48. He had moved up the previous summer with his girlfriend, a friendly woman who had left two kids with her ex-husband in California and quickly gotten work at the local bakery. By midwinter, she had gone back. She sold her skis to me before she left. The A-frame's metal roof sloped down nearly to the ground, making the place dark and look a bit like a silo. Two other homes shared the gravel road: a wood-sided house surrounded by spruce that was built by a fisherman who came up from Colorado to fish during the summer, and a two-story round house being built—and lived in—by a young couple with a collie who walked into their place (or traveled by snowshoe in the winter) the quarter-mile from where they parked on the edge of the road.

We continued westward, under a white sky which afforded the kind of muted, directionless light that made seeing subtle topography in the snow difficult. There were so many different kinds of snow for skiing. In early winter, heavy powder layered in the hills, and you sank almost to your knees. In the spring, a clean icy crust often formed on the surface of the snow; you could careen across it at high speeds, but gaining purchase to make a turn was difficult. The best was a combination— a crust with a few inches of fresh snow for a soft, clean glide, and a bit of cushioning if you fell. But by afternoon, we would likely pierce through the crust. As the day warmed, it would cave in, but this late in the season, the snow had settled and we wouldn't sink in far.

John and I skied side by side. I loved to feel every muscle in my body strain and then stretch itself out with each stride. I could feel the backs of my thighs and upper arms, my stomach and calves all pushing to get ahead. The only sounds were of our skis gliding across the snow, the poles puncturing the crust, the squeak of our boots against their bindings and the rush of our exhalations. Sweat was forming on my forehead beneath my wool hat, under the waistband of my pants, and between my gloves and the palms of my hands. I stopped to unzip my coat, remove layers, and catch my breath. Up ahead, John flew down a hill, his maroon windbreaker opening like wings under his arms. When he fell at the bottom, his skis sliding out from under him, he laughed and then lay back in the snow to take a break. I relished the sensation of full-body exhaustion I would feel by evening, and pressed on to catch up with him.

We skied downhill through spruce and across the deep, cloven pocks left by moose. In a couple of months, moose would come into town to drop their calves. Photos of young calves born in people's backyards would appear on the front pages of the two local newspapers. Their over-sized heads, miniature horselike bodies, and spindly legs seemed illogically proportioned. By midsummer, most of the moose moved back into the hills. In the fall or winter bulls shed their antlers, which were often hidden by snow until spring. As we skied into the creek drainage, the snow broke open in places, revealing deep black seams where water ran darkly five feet below us. The sound of running water, which was normally absent in the winter landscape, was evidence that things were starting to wake up again.

SOMETIMES THE FIRST snow flew long before Halloween. In other years, cold rain pierced us long into November.

But when winter came in Alaska, it made the landscape bloom again. On clear, cold mornings, crystals blossomed on the surface of the snow, catching the sun like peach fuzz on young skin. Hoarfrost petaled the dead, saucer-sized umbels of pushki that still stood shoulder-high out of the snow, and ice sprouted like asters along hollow fireweed stalks. Icicles dropped glistening taproots from the edges of roofs, and on bare patches beneath spruce, ice crystals extended like vines. Snow made spruce trees look as if they had grown new white boughs on top of the old. Along the beach, frost spread like a gardener's groundcover among the cobbles. Sometimes snowflakes dropped from the sky like cherry blossoms set to the wind and you could catch these flowers in your mouth. Other times, snow left a dust as fine as pollen.

As a kid, I had longed for snow, knowing that just the threat of it—an inch or two predicted for that afternoon—could cancel school. A dozen miles outside the nation's capital, snow and ice meant that everyone was worried about getting sued. But I had noticed very little about the snow itself—all I cared about was whether it was sticky, which meant good snowball fight conditions. Here, snow reinvented the landscape. After months of fall darkness, when we lost more than a half hour of daylight in a single week, the first snowfall whitewashed everything. The snow damped noise, silencing the grumble of the trucks we heard all summer long. Gray clouds piled into the bay and dropped flakes so silently all you could hear was a gentle static that seemed like the absence of sound. Snow insulated houses, blocking drafts and layering heavily onto roofs where it trapped warmth. Around town, winter brought an incessant falling and melting of snow. Cottony clouds gripped the top of the bluff behind town, then let go, having powdered the brown hills as white as talc. Snow made everything shipshape. All of those messy in-between areas—vacant lots around town, yards filled with parts cars, horse trailers, rusting trucks, stacked fishing gear—looked neater after they were dressed in a starch-white snow.

The drastic changes each season wreaked on the landscape forced people to think about making drastic changes of their own. Some decided to take off in the winter for life in a hot climate. Others downsized, upgraded, cut their hair, got a divorce. Over the course of the year, the land around us morphed from bloom, to green, to brown, to white. Six feet of growth died back to nothing and then was replaced by head-high snow. The different selves emerged: the melancholy, the manic, the purposeful, the lazy.

Although the changes winter brought to coastal Alaska were extreme, the season here was much milder than in the Interior. The sea, which absorbs and releases the sun's heat slowly, tempers the extremes of summer and winter. As the days shorten and the temperatures drop in the fall, the sea cools more slowly than the land, keeping coastal areas mild. By late winter, the temperature of the sea drops to its lowest point, and as the days lengthen and the sunlight increases in intensity, the cold ocean cools coastal regions.

Although true celestial mid-summer and mid-winter occur on the solstices, the sea's sluggish pace of storing and giving off heat helps cause the bulk of cold winter days to come after the shortest day of the year and summer's warmth to run long after summer solstice. In Homer, winter temperatures rarely dropped below zero, but the tempering influence of the sea faded in the higher elevations even a couple of miles from town, where temperatures were often significantly colder and winter lasted a month longer. And just ninety miles up the highway in more inland communities, you could count on the temperature being ten degrees colder in the winter and ten degrees warmer in the summer. But each winter erased the memory of the one before. At the end of every winter, people around town agreed that it had been the coldest, the mildest, the sloppiest, the driest, or the most rainy winter ever.

Although the sea dampened the extremes of winter, the beach was magical during the frozen months. By morning, hoarfrost had wrapped each beach cobble individually, and as the day passed, sunlight melted the ice on the south faces of the stones until each dark cobble was merely capped with white. Then the tide came in and painted the beach black again. Ice crystals powdered seaweed on the beach and froze it into solid gnarls. Creeks that normally spilled across the beach froze into shelves of ice, and seeps along the bluff shellacked the dusty earth. During the coldest weather, high tides quietly deposited shoulder-high continents of sea ice at the top of the beach and slushy waves rolled in languidly.

In the middle of winter, the harbor, generally free of ice, was quiet. No tourists piled onto boats to be shuttled out to catch salmon or halibut. Commercial fishing boats rested in their slips. The fish packing plant went silent after the holiday season of sending gifts of frozen seafood all over the country. Most of the businesses on the Spit— bear viewing outfits, water taxis, the ice cream shop, espresso and trinket stands—closed, and many boarded up their windows with plywood to wait out the winter.

After the flush of summer, Homer's population seemed to halve in the winter, but the dark months created pockets of vibrancy. Businesses strung lights along their roofs and around nearby trees. The community college in Homer showed foreign films for free on Friday evenings, and restaurants offered weeknight dinner specials that weren't available during the summer months— half-priced burgers, fish and chips, clam chowder. The six-month-long winter passed through town in a succession of annual events and scheduled celebrations: the craft fair that coincided with the annual community production of *The Nutcracker*, the winter arts festival which was accompanied by a parade down the main thoroughfare through town, a dozen fundraisers for various causes, and skiing competitions for all ages.

Supermarkets around town maintained their earnest stocks of colorful produce even when the ground was frozen and the sun had slumped low in the sky. The same waxy apples were flown in from the other side of the globe, bananas were shipped north from the tropics, and heads of sensitive lettuce were brought up from California. All winter long, we emptied our freezer of salmon we'd caught the summer before. We grilled it, fried it, baked it, and put it into soups. We ate salmon for dinner, then brought leftovers to work for lunch. We ate the raspberries we'd made into jam and syrup late in the summer and used up the clams we'd canned as chowder. By late winter, the berries and clams were gone and we were sick of salmon.

Winter brought its own recreation. When the town's largest lake, which was used during the summer months as the floatplane airport, was frozen fast, people raced beat-up cars across its surface. Scores of snowmachiners parked their trucks and trailers a dozen miles out the road that headed east from town and took off into the wide expanse of undeveloped backcountry. Ice rinks sprang up—a flooded blacktop next to the elementary school, a frozen pond next to the airport—and attracted skaters who gathered to twirl, do laps, and play hockey. As we skated across its surface, the pond let out haunting sounds like the calls of whales. Three sets of trails were groomed around Homer for cross-country skiers. Years before John and I moved there, a group of fishermen had put up a rope tow on Ohlson Mountain, a stout hill behind town, using a boat engine to drag skiers up the slope.

As you travel north during an Alaskan winter, the sun slinks lower and lower toward the horizon until you reach the Arctic Circle at 66° latitude, which runs across the state about two-thirds of the way to its northern coast. There, the sun doesn't rise at all on winter solstice. If you took a dogsled north from that dotted line on the map, you'd lose the sun for days, then weeks, then months. In Alaska and other northern regions, the wide arc the sun makes across the northern sky all summer long is pulled taut, until the sun merely scrapes low along the southern horizon. The moon usurps the sun's summer path and dominates the winter sky. The winter constellations I'd learned the year before returned. Orion led the parade across winter's night skies; W-shaped Cassiopeia, her husband Cepheus, the Great Square, and that small question mark–shaped group of seven stars called the Pleiades followed suit. Here, it was easy to see how the sky rotates around the North Star, which sits almost directly above the Earth's axis: Over the course of one night, the Big Dipper dumped itself out. A clear moonless night revealed a sky infinitely perforated by stars and in the morning, Venus glowed so brightly it cast its own milky light on the surface of the bay.

But the dark sky had once again ratcheted around us. The darkness drove us home earlier on winter afternoons, and kept us in later in the mornings. Before moving to Alaska, I had been warned about the long, dark winters. John and I had looked up the statistics for Homer: The shortest day of the year—December 21, winter solstice— offered about six hours of light. The sun rose at 10:05 A.M. and set at 4:04 P.M. The darkness had seemed mysterious and exciting. But we hadn't known that the *qual-*

*ity* of light also changed drastically with the seasons. Because the Northern Hemisphere leans away from the sun during the winter months, in midwinter the sun rises barely a hand's width above the mountain range to the south. Shadows are long even at midday. In winter, sunlight passes through a band of light-scattering atmosphere thicker than at any other time of year, which makes the light gentle and hazy. Over the radio, experts urged listeners to go outside during the few lighted hours in order to get at least twenty minutes of sunlight into our retinas each day, which they said would help ward off depression from seasonal affective disorder. Shops around town sold lights that simulated the sun, some of which steadily brightened, like a plug-in dawn.

Although neither John nor I seemed to be suffering from lack of light, winter forced us to look at ourselves and at each other, and it wasn't just because the view out our windows disappeared for so much of the day. For more hours than not, the panes framed reflections of ourselves. John pulled out his book on the stars, which suggested what it called a new way of seeing the constellations—new pictures to link stars, new ways to connect the dots. Given the same dozen points, you could draw so many different things. I began to think of all of the lives I could live: up north at the edge of the sea or someplace else; with or without John; as a teacher, student, or as someone else entirely. The points in my life could be reshuffled to create different, overlapping lives, in the same way stars are shared between constellations: The end of the Dipper's handle becomes the nose of Ursus Major. Andromeda's head is also one of the corners of the Great Square.

I couldn't help it. I began to slip into these other lives, as you might for a moment stop seeing the ladle and see only the bear. I imagined curling up on the couch with the friendly plow guy when he came into the house to use the phone when John was gone. The plow guy had gotten his truck stuck in the ditch along the driveway. Why hadn't I told him that there was a ditch there, now hidden under the snow? Didn't I know that was my job? My stupidity made me cringe, but the plow guy, in work pants wet up to the thigh from wading into the snow, was gentle and unfazed. I considered taking off to learn tango in Argentina, where it was summer. I would throw on a flimsy dress and slide into a pair of heels. Or I would leave and go back to school. Perhaps being a student would cure me of the incessant feeling that I was an apprentice of my own life. Sometimes all I wanted was to escape the way I felt when John looked at me: as his perpetual student, the girl in overalls and rubber boots ready to accompany him on his next adventure. But it didn't take long for the familiar pictures to resurface, the Dipper to return, Orion's shield to weld together its line of stars.

LESS THAN A mile from the house, our skis slipped quickly into the icy dips in the snow beneath spruce trees. We crossed undeveloped parcels owned by people who lived out of state. We'd never seen anyone here, though our neighbors told us that in the spring, they picked morels in these fields. We had the expanse of snow and scattered spruce woods to ourselves. Winter could be like this: moments of intense intimacy with others—shared dinners in small spaces with friends and cheap wine, bodies packed into someone's sauna, crowds gathered at the few restaurants open in town—and then whole days when John and I would see no one else. But in the quiet of winter, snow revealed the industry of hundreds of silent societies. Highways of vole tracks careened between clumps of elderberry, and moose crashed across the hills, leaving beheaded willows in their wakes. The telltale prints of snowshoe hares—with their huge hind paws landing ahead of their diminutive forelegs—traversed the snow, followed by lynx tracks as large as saucers. Coyotes left curious, winding trails, and squirrels dropped nervous, claw-scratched tracks. And even the wings of an owl swooping down to pluck off a meal left a gentle swipe.

The bears had gone into hibernation; the shorebirds and warblers had gone south, but life was everywhere. Hummingbird-sized golden-crowned kinglets, olive green birds with a brilliant streak of yellow across the tops of their heads, dashed between spruce branches all winter long. We were amazed that they could survive the cold months in the north. They nested around town in the summer, and in the spring, we heard their earnest, energetic calls, like a car engine turning over again and again but never starting. Ravens traversed the white winter sky, chortling to each other on the wing. A crow-sized hawk owl perched regularly at the top of a spruce tree near the fast-food joint. Magpies, whose black and white plumage reflected winter's simple palette, flapped around town. Snow buntings examined grasses on the berm at the top of the beach, and huge flocks of redpolls—small brown songbirds with bright spots of red on the tops of their heads—chutted by overhead, then congregated momentarily in stands of alders.

In the winter, the bay, which remained open in all but the most protected areas, provided a haven for tanker ships as well as seabirds. Ducks rafted up in great numbers. From the beach we could see the white flanks of scaup gathered by the hundreds, the black profiles of clumped scoters, pairs of goldeneyes, single grebes, and drab loons diving in the shallows near the edge of the surf. Otters gathered in the bay as well, and seals periscoped their heads through the cold surface of the sea just off the beach in town.

For those species that didn't migrate, winter up north required innovation. The hares replaced their dingy brown summer coats with fur of unblemished white composed of hollow hairs that insulated the animals from the winter chill. Moose grew thick coats that would peel away messily in the spring. In the fall, spruce grouse gathered on gravel roads to fill their gizzards with grit to help them digest their winter diet of stiff spruce needles. The frogs we heard calling in the spring hibernated in burrows of dead leaves and grasses, sleeping beneath thick layers of snow.

Winter meant a peculiar mixture of quietness and life, of darkness and earnest vibrancy, of accessibility and danger. For John and me, winter proved to be an equalizing season. For eight months, I could forget about my fear of the water. Winter was a terrain I felt comfortable in. We stored our boats and explored the land instead of the sea. I was more adept as a skier than John, and I wasn't afraid of the cold. I learned quickly how to dress for a ski trip: Wear far less than what seemed rationally appropriate. In cold temperatures, sweat can be dangerous. Once wet, your body can lose heat rapidly. I wasn't afraid of getting lost, either; beyond the familiar scattering of houses, the land creased into shallow valleys holding creeks that all ran, faster or slower, toward the same narrow river, and soon after to the sea. There were no tiderips to plan around, no clues in the surface of the sea to pick up on. By midwinter, the topography behind our place was etched in my brain: Twitter Creek ran by Lookout Mountain; Beaver Creek Flats would take you to the North Fork of the Anchor; Crossman Ridge humped up between our place and Ohlson Mountain.

As friends and family back East repeatedly asked me how I was handling the long winter, I realized I had become sensitive to the subtleties of the season: the acute angle of light, the way fresh animal tracks in the snow dulled during the days after they were laid, the red hue cast by thick stands of leafless alders. Summer was why people came here, but winter was why many of us stayed.

But lately, you couldn't count on winter. Friends who

had lived in Alaska for years lamented the recent whimsy of winter. You couldn't depend on there being good snow anymore, they complained. That winter, Iditarod dog mushers were forced to cross fifty miles of bare ground— their sleds bounced over tussocks and brush in an area usually blanketed by snow. The previous winter, racers worried that the unusually warm winter temperatures— in the upper thirties—would overheat and dehydrate their dogs. Frequent news reports suggested that the typical deep freeze of Alaska's winters was no longer a sure thing. On Alaska's Arctic oil fields, winter freeze-up allowed massive machinery to travel off the network of gravel roads that linked the scattered drill pads and processing facilities. But this season of ice roads was getting shorter, threatening the slow-growing tundra beneath the heavy equipment. Each winter, the tiny, half-Native Interior village of Nenana held a competition in which people all over the world guessed when the village's river would break up. The jackpot of about $300,000 was shared by those who guessed the right date, hour, and minute. The river was now breaking up, on average, five and a half days earlier than it had in 1917, when the contest was initiated by railroad workers itching for spring. Late winters and early springs made travel more difficult and even deadly in the Bush: Snowmachines and trucks sometimes crashed through thin ice in places where villagers had once been able to rely upon safe passage. Warming temperatures were unraveling winter's fabric.

ON OUR SKIS, we continued downstream beyond where the creek joined another. There was no one around but the old zipperlike tracks of snowmachines fading in the creek bottom. From time to time they'd highmark their machines, driving up steep sides of the drainage in daredevil loops. In the backcountry, these routes could kill snowmachiners because they triggered avalanches. Up ahead, a series of beaver dams hemmed ice-covered pools. The pools drained into a reservoir that held the town's drinking water.

I stopped on my skis when I spotted a caddisfly crawling across the snow. These half inch-long insects wear wings tented above their brown bodies. The sight of this fragile creature crawling across the wide expanse of snow was a reminder that spring, eventually, would come. As larvae, caddisflies live in cold and swift-running creeks, wearing elaborate homes they've pieced together out of twigs and pebbles. They spin nets to catch food, and when they're fully grown, the larvae close themselves in their houses and begin the first stages of metamorphosis. In early spring, the insects crawl out of the water, and step out of their old skins wearing new wings. Then they mate, lay eggs, and die. Would this one, emerging so early, find a mate?

I called to John and he skied over to where I watched the insect moving slowly across the snow. We both loved to find wild things where you wouldn't expect them, and to notice what could easily be overlooked. In front of us, ice lidded a shallow pond. We took off our skis at the edge and then inched our boots onto its startlingly clear surface. The ice was as transparent as glass. We lay flat on our bellies and looked through the hard surface. The ice was a window into another world, showing the pond's winter life. Brown grasses danced in the invisible current, which carried silver air bubbles along the underside of the ice ceiling. Larval caddisflies stepped gingerly along submerged leaves and black beetles zipped about in the frigid water wearing pockets of air like glimmering skirts. A white worm wiggled through the water among the stumps of last year's horsetails.

The ice was part window, part mirror. The surface reflected my face, which was framed by the white of the sky and the black, sawlike tops of spruce behind my head. My hair brushed the ice; I touched my lips to its cold surface and then my tongue. The taste was metallic and clean.

Every time I thought about the other lives I could live, I remembered this: What existed between John and me was a penchant for hidden worlds, for moments of extraordinary beauty. For seeing the way mist hung in the valley below our place, the way a moose would steam on a cold fall morning, the way a full winter moon rose swollen over the mountains. Every time I thought about the other places I could be, I thought about the endless snow-covered hills we seemed to own on weekend days in late winter, the evidence of lynx. Still, I wondered whether life would always feel so tentative and uncertain. Whether I would always imagine living other lives. But winter was my territory, and in it, I was the woman who could put skis on in the morning and leave the house not knowing where she'd end up.

# 9

# SPRING

CAT'S PAW: *n. A puff of wind; a light breeze affecting a small area, as one that causes patches of ripples on the surface of a water area.*

In the spring, the landscape got dirty again. All winter long, each new layer of snow had licked clean the hills behind town. Foot upon foot had fallen, smoothing the hummocks that stubbled open fields, tidying up the valleys, erasing last year's drooped grasses from the endless slopes. Now, wind and rain and days that promised five more minutes of light than the day before were quietly undoing all of that. A winter's worth of flotsam surfaced: a dropped glove, a garden spade forgotten in the yard, the root ball of a dead houseplant tossed out the front door months before. Over a weekend, the picnic table buoyed up in the front yard, afloat on a draining sea. Spruce trees flung needles that looked like dark fingernail clippings across the surface of the snow and shed tangles of black lichen from their branches. The clean expanse of snow became a mess.

At this time of year, it became clear that every object held heat among its swimming atoms: Deep moats formed around the bases of spruce trees where the dark trunks, having absorbed the sun's gentle warmth, melted the snow away. A single piece of gravel pushed off the road by the plow months before would melt the snow around it as a drop of soap scatters an oily film. Gardeners threw ash atop their snow-covered beds, and these sooty patches, taking in more heat than the reflective ground around them, would be denuded first.

Land was on the move. You could stand in the middle of a snow-coated meadow and hear the crackling of melting ice and the slurring of water first seeping then running downgrade to find more of itself. Having been locked up for months, water was eager to pool, to mingle. It ran in every ditch, in every drainage, and gathered itself in every hollow. It needed to move, to transgress boundaries and flood fences. A certain kind of school was letting out for the rush of melt, then of summer. Finally rivers and streams were able to hear the sounds of their own voices again and remember what it felt like to fall downstream, to enter the sea. It was a phase change: solid to liquid; nothing was spared.

Everything else was on the move too. Moose roved into town from the hills, where deep snow made passage difficult for these long-legged animals. They moved between the edges of parking lots and vacant parcels, browsing on willows and the tips of spruce. Sea ducks that had wintered on open water returned and flecked the bay in black.

Warblers dashed in and then proceeded to sing for hours from the boughs of birches, cottonwoods, and alders that would soon leaf out. In a matter of days, moths crowded the air and, at night, headlights waded into their midst. Nighttime itself was going someplace else.

It was late April, and the snow was rotten and patchy, strewn with debris and pulpy in places. The skiing was no good. There hadn't been fresh snow in weeks. The tops of willows poked through. I wanted spring to get on with itself. I folded myself onto the couch with a book while John set off to work on a project, digging out our wooden kayaks we'd stored in the fall so that we could get on the water before the snow was completely gone, which might not be until June.

Months earlier, to protect our boats from winter weather, we had slid them side by side in the crawl space beneath the floor of an unfinished building our land-lord had started the year before. The plywood surface extended twenty by twenty feet and would, the landlord planned, support a building that was part of a business scheme he talked about from time to time. He would turn the house into a retreat center and build outbuildings where dozens of people could sleep. Already there was a similar structure on the property as well as an outhouse and part of a ropes course. The landlord had stashed his own fleet of a half-dozen brightly-colored plastic kay-aks—also part of the business plan—in this spot as well, to protect them from the feet of snow that would fall over the course of the winter.

That afternoon, the boats had been far from my mind. I didn't want to think about making the crossing to the other side of the bay. I didn't want to think about having to read the water, navigate the tide rips. A winter of skiing the hills behind our place had ruined me—the predictable swells of land, the gentle current of one drainage running into another; slack was when you stood still on your skis and took a break. It was a form of subtle protest, my reading on the couch. I didn't want to help. I wanted to linger in the terrestrial world for as long as I could, but John was determined to get up and go.

Sometimes I found John's endless energy exhausting. In his eyes, there was always another project to do. And the moment he'd arrived in Alaska, his dream came into focus: to explore the state's wildest places by its waterways. Reluctantly, I agreed that this seemed the best way to approach it. John ordered the kit for my boat soon after. But building the boat wasn't the only thing there was to do; we would also have to refinish the wood every year or two; maintain paddles, life vests, and safety equipment; acquire maps and charts; and constantly glean advice from people with more experience.

Two pages from the end of the chapter I was reading, John burst back through the front door. "Something's wrong with the boats!" He was out of breath from sprinting back to the house. "I need a light for a better look." He ran to the closet to get a headlamp, leaving torn waffle-shaped pieces of snow fallen from the tread of his boots melting on the wood floor. I jumped off the couch, grabbed a jacket, yanked on my rubber boots, and followed him out the front door to the side of the house where the platform was encircled by spruce. More than half a dozen feet of snow had fallen that winter, piling up heavily on every flat surface.

When we got to the clearing, I could see that drifts had piled up higher than the level of the building's floor, and John had taken a shovel to the solid, six-foot bank to create a space through which we could drag out our kayaks. But after a few minutes of shoveling, he realized something wasn't right. When he'd cleared enough snow away to reveal the edge of the building's floor, he saw that it tilted up toward the sky. The structure had collapsed.

WHEN THE SNOW melted away, the world of human things rose up: hastily thrown-up cabins, trailers long forgotten, yard junk. The garden patch that had looked tidy for months under snow revealed the knotted mess of pea vines and bolted radish heads you hadn't bothered to pull in the fall. It was time to work the beds and start seeds. Time to change out your car tires and pick up a winter's worth of blown trash. It was time to weed through your closets and bring what you no longer used down to the Pick 'n' Pay, where your neighbor could buy your old shirt back for a quarter. Spring begged for work—so much needed to be cleaned up, prepared. But that afternoon, I didn't want to budge.

In the middle of spring chores, you realized the

enormous amount of time spent acquiring stuff and then taking care of it. Some people joked about how many motors they had to keep running: two cars, an old plow truck, a boat, lawn mower, four-wheeler, and a generator just in case. This didn't include the fridge, oil heater fan, and well pump. Just the sheer number of shoes needed to get by in winter was astounding: rubber boots for wet days, snow boots for cold ones, ski boots, ice skates, inside shoes for work, slippers for the cold floor at home. Life here required a new set of possessions I gradually acquired—things I would never use if I moved almost anywhere else: clam shovel, sturdy down parka, a collection of five-gallon plastic buckets, rebar cut into garden post-lengths, jars for pickling fish in, an assortment of fishing nets for various purposes, scrap wood, milk crates, and hardware salvaged from the dump. I accumulated and collected; sometimes it all seemed like too much junk.

But there was a culture of junk here, and a few locals were lauded and despised for their exceptional ability, or tendency, to accumulate it. Les Wilson owned one of the most beautiful parcels around: thirty-nine sunny acres of meadow, birch, and some live spruce. His property, about three miles out of town, was flat, perfect for farming, tending a nice grassy yard, or just lying down in the meadow when the fireweed was aflame and staring up at the sky. He'd bought the place a decade before for a price that would make local subdividers salivate, and then began covering it with junk. Now it was a compound of the neglected, a community of odds and ends. A muddy loop road across the property ringed his stockpiles of junk: propane tanks, old cars, trucks, camper vans, stacks of car door panels, beer cans, tires, steel beams, welder's tanks, buoys, blue tarps. Les had hauled in a few dilapidated trailers salvaged from someplace else that he dropped in rows at the edge of the mud road and rented out for too much money. There were a couple of hand-built cabins occupied by men who helped Les continue carting stuff in. You could look at it as a sign of resourcefulness and industry. Someday he might be able to provide for someone in need—and that's what kept him going. But you could also see it as a scab on the land, an insult, even a tragedy. The planes to and from Anchorage flew over the place half a dozen times a day. The view from above—of junk creeping into untouched meadow, pooling up around birch trees—was not pretty.

But salvage, Les said, was part of the Alaskan mentality. Living for years far from stores and supply shops, off the road system or during the days before a highway and town rose up around you, you learned to keep stuff, to scrimp, save, and be resourceful. "That's not a junk car," he philosophized, "that's the parts for the car you're driving." Why get rid of something—even an eyesore—when someday you, or your neighbor, or a guy with some cash in his wallet, might want it? "I'm not in it to get rich," Les declared. He realized that wasn't likely going to happen, of course, but for him, piling up junk—living off the opulent bycatch of our lives—seemed a higher calling.

Over the years, the city council had made numerous rules about junk. What would happen if the whole town were cleaned up? No derelict boats out on the Spit. No junk cars in people's yards. We could be as spotless a tourist destination as Disney World. But there were quiet incentives to the contrary. Space wasn't much of a limiting factor, so there was always room for more junk, even though the landfill, barely two miles out of town, accepted almost anything for free. And outside city limits, people could do just about anything with their properties: gravel mine, airstrip, dog yards.

A junkyard here or there was no big deal. We could handle it. Things were worse in the Bush, far off the road system, where nearly everything was flown or barged in—televisions, generators, snowmachines, refrigerators, sofas—and nearly everything stayed. "Combi" jets heading to hub communities off the road system had half of their fuselages blocked off for cargo. Passengers sat in the aft section of the plane behind a bulkhead on the other side of which sat cases of soda, stereos, and power tools.

A new school arrived in pieces by the planeload to a remote village: lumber, metal roofing, nails, sacks of concrete. But Bush life depended on air transport for more than just bringing in stuff. "You see the whole cycle of life," a pilot explained. "You haul a young guy to a village where there's a girl waiting for him. Then you haul the wedding party. Then you haul the young mom with a new baby." He added, "You fly Grandpa out to the hospital when he's sick and then his body back to his village to be buried."

Dealing with solid waste is a tricky problem in the Bush. Plumbing has come slowly to rural Alaska, which means that residents in many Native villages collected their waste in honey buckets lined with plastic bags. The plastic bags were then dumped into a lagoon dug out of the ground a short distance from the village. I had flown over communities where you could see the blue bags slopped into these shallow pits. Honey buckets presented a public health disaster, and millions of state and federal dollars were being pumped into the Bush to build water and sewer systems. But in many cases, not enough money was socked away for maintaining these systems, which are extraordinarily expensive to build and operate because of months of subzero temperatures, extensive waterlogged ground, and permafrost. One village, facing a decade-long project with a price tag of $43 million just to plumb its two hundred homes, turned to raising funds through pull-tab gambling.

Most villages dumped trash in open landfills. On weekends, people went there for spare parts. Making junk go away, out of sight in a flat, treeless landscape, was expensive or impossible. Why shouldn't used cars be dumped along a river in hopes they'd shore up an eroding bank? Well-meaning people were arranging empty DC-10s to fly steadily accumulating junk out of the Bush to scrapyards and recyclers in Anchorage and as far away as Seattle. In one year, more than a million pounds of used cars. Alaska's most remote places had become sinks not only for trash, an insult to the eyes, but worse, to the invisible jetsam of modern life: toxins leaking from landfills, radioactive materials on abandoned military sites, pollutants from other parts of the world that collected in the north as if it were a giant river eddy. We couldn't see this trash, but knew it littered our lives.

But in town, most of us wanted the lifestyle here we'd known elsewhere. We wanted wine, food from far away, books, clothes we liked. Two companies delivered nearly all of the cargo that came into the state, which arrived by ship at the Anchorage port. A single ship of the four that arrived weekly could pour out two hundred cars. Vast quantities of construction materials were shipped up to erect structures to hold other stuff. Machines and materials came in ships to be trucked north to Arctic tundra oil fields. Tons of groceries arrived every week by ship because so little food was grown instate. I tried to picture just the number of bananas shipped north each week. Shipping companies operated on a policy to keep eight days' worth of food on store shelves or in transit. People were beginning to recognize the disaster that would ensue if a link fell off the chain, but, despite the state's independent mindset, we were becoming more reliant on staples—on milk, eggs, bread, and everything else—from hundreds and thousands of miles away.

Alaska produces almost nothing; the ships come up full and leave mostly empty, except during summer when they cart seafood away. Each day is a parade of stuff into the state: doughnuts, sneakers, car tires, lumber. As the snow melted away that spring, the question rung out: Where did it all end up? Landfills swelled, backyards filled, warehouses restocked, houses shot up on cleared slopes.

In early summer, it was hard not to detest the arrival of so much equipment: RVs the size of eighteen-wheelers towing shiny SUVs, trailers spilling out four-wheelers, trucks trailering thirty-foot fishing boats. Like seeds set to the breeze, tents were strewn across the Spit, sprouting fire pits, parked rental cars, driftwood and tarp structures that struggled against the wind. Each year, a few took root and stayed.

It was impossible to resist the urge to surround ourselves with what we knew, what we owned, what we bought and created. Recently, I'd complained to John about not having a spot for my books, the few knick-knacks I'd brought with me or recently accumulated. When I'd moved to Alaska, I had abandoned my meager amount of furniture—scrounged from yard sales and friends—and instead brought only what I could carry in a backpack and two bags I'd loaded onto the ferry. With so few things of my own around, life felt transitory, like a rental. So, I started collecting: rocks shaped like squares, small gray beach pebbles smoothed by the sea, gull verte-brae scrubbed by surf, driftwood sculpted into pleasing forms. I covered the windowsills and wanted more space. I thought if I had my own spot for my own things, it might make my life here seem less provisional. Over the winter, John had encouraged me to build a small bookshelf using the landlord's shop and scrap wood he'd salvaged. John showed me how to use a table saw, circular saw, jigsaw, and router. The shelf emerged as a stunted piece of furni-ture, made to fit below a window, and impractically short for anyplace else. I'd get rid of the shelf a few years later, another piece of junk that moved through my hands and then out of sight.

If you thought about it long enough, it could make you weep or feel sick to your stomach: We were ruining the very thing we'd all moved here for. We were bringing in so much stuff, our footprint was always spreading into places where no human development had existed before. We were clearing land for more refuse: for buildings that would rot away within a generation or two; for level land on which to park cars that would eventually break down and fall apart; to raise up storage units to hold things we rarely used. Developers felled trees, scraped the rolling landscape flat, subdivided, hauled in truckloads of gravel for an access road, and planted a sign: PANORAMIC VISTA: NATURE OUT YOUR FRONT DOOR.

As with life anywhere else, the rubble of our lives held our histories. You couldn't give Dungeness crab or shrimp pots away anymore, so they piled in yards as evidence of busted fisheries, an ocean changing faster than people's ability to forget. A mechanical clam digger with wheels more than six feet high sat rusting in the mudflats on the Spit for years. Originally a military vehicle used to haul equipment across snow, it had been outfitted to dig into sand for razor clams as part of a pilot commercial clamming project that went belly-up. When the city launched a beautification project that encouraged people to haul away junk, a local machinist who had snuck beers with friends behind the massive digger during high school dragged the thing eight miles out the road to his front yard. One day, he planned, he would turn it into a snow-roving rig again, complete with cab, heat, and tunes, and set up to haul broken-down snowmachines out of the backcountry, or at least he would salvage its steel frame. The *Double Eagle*, a sixty-five-foot wooden boat built out of cypress and used off the Gulf Coast as a shrimper was brought up during the *Exxon Valdez* oil spill to assist with cleanup efforts and afterward, sat in the boatyard for a decade peeling paint. People said it had been used as a brothel during the cleanup, when hundreds of men lined up for high-paying jobs doing work that was too little, too late. The big boat was a reminder of our clumsiness, waste-fulness, and constant hunger.

Our middens exposed us—the clamshells we tossed under a shrub in the yard, the refuse we left at the dump: In the future, these would tell stories about us. Some-day, they would be sorted through, decoded. I was afraid of what they would say. These accumulations of things tied us down. Sometimes they remembered too much. Sometimes we needed to break away, to cast off and start afresh. Each year, we watched it happen before our eyes: Trees dropped their leaves to save up for new ones; ducks molted their flight feathers and waited flightless for new primaries; the bay scraped its beaches clean and started over. Sometimes I wanted to do the same: swipe every last stone and shell from the windowsills and chuck them into the yard; toss every knickknack that was some relic of the past; take off through the front door with a backpack and just walk away alone. But it was easier to stay put; there was comfort in the clutter. On the days when the ugly mess of our daily lives grew too much, the view across the water was a necessary distraction. We oriented ourselves to the south.

THE FLOOR HAD been built about three feet off the ground and was completely buried by snow. John had already begun to dig along the structure's north side, and we shoveled together quickly until we hit the pocket of snowlessness beneath the structure so we could get a look at the boats. John put the headlamp on, lay on his belly on the snow, and stuck his head through. "My boat's totaled," he said calmly. "I don't know about yours." We continued to dig until we were up to our middles in a trench along the north side of the platform, and then we crawled below the edge of the sunken structure. It took a few seconds for my eyes to adjust to the darkness beneath the floor; the snow made everything bright everywhere else. But then what lay below the failed structure came into focus: A floor joist had fallen through the deck of my kayak, splitting it like taut skin. The gash was ragged, the torn edge raw and unfinished. The two-by-twelve supporting beam that held up the edge of the floor had cracked around the bolt that held it in place. A collection of fissures below the bolt formed the perfect outline of a horse's head in the wood. I couldn't remember what my boat had looked like before. My memory of its perfectly gleaming deck was instantly erased.

John's boat, too, had been broken in half; a joist pierced its white hull. It looked like a compound fracture. We were wading through the silent wreckage of it all as the snow slowly melted around the edge of the floor. The collapse could have happened weeks ago; we would never know. Now, there was only the still scene of disaster: varnished plywood—millimeters thin—punctured; joists snapped; pressboard failed. It was such a waste.

There was nothing to do with the boats but burn them. We slid the kayaks out of storage through the hole we dug in the snow, then we threw them onto a pile of spruce stumps in the yard, poured some gasoline on top, and set it alight. I had to watch. I stood on the snow in the yard staring at the air watery with heat and the stream of smoke being bullied about by switching breezes. The smell of burning gas lingered; the fire warmed my face, chest, the fronts of my legs. As the flames gathered around the remains of my boat, a sheet of silvery white fiberglass cloth, which had covered the entire kayak lifted off the broken wooden form like a ghost, hovering for a moment in the air before collapsing back into the fire which smoldered around it ineffectually for hours. Over the course of the afternoon, the heat of the bonfire fingered into the snow around it, melting it into parallel ridges that radiated around the fire. Dozens of feet away from the flames, the burn left a record in the snow.

As soon as the burnpile cooled, John shaved his beard

clean and began building a new kayak. I had never seen his bare face before, his thin upper lip or the expanse of skin between his nose and mouth. He looked like someone I didn't know. It was like erasing a memory and suddenly creating a new one. In six weeks, the new boat was done and John carried it outside into the yard, where the grass was now almost completely green. He lowered himself into the cockpit, rocking the boat on its keel and feeling it hold him at the hips. John wanted nothing but to get it in the water and go. And soon he would. But later that afternoon, with the boat still under the sun on the grass, a bull moose lumbered into the yard to gnaw on an elderberry shrub steps away from John's new boat. We watched nervously from the window, afraid to startle the animal lest it put a hoof through the deck. The moose lost interest and moved on.

There are seasons in life when things seem to disappear. That was one of those seasons. The boats gone, the snow, John's beard, a black cat with a white bib we'd adopted from the pound in the fall who didn't come home one day. Picked off by a hawk or coyote, we assumed. The landscape naked of snow was bony and sullen, sallow and emptied out. Beneath our feet, the earth was waterlogged and cold; it waited.

In a few weeks, John would find the single picture he'd taken of me in my boat on its maiden voyage. You couldn't tell it was me, the image was so small. But you could see the slick gleam of the boat on the surface of the bay, a slice reflecting the sun. He put it in a frame and set it on the windowsill. Now I could brag about the accomplishment of building it, but didn't have to face the responsibility of owning it, or the obligation to explore by sea. I felt an indefinable sense of relief—one that I could never share with John. I hated that sense of relief, but knew it was true. A tie to this place, to this man, had come undone.

# 10

# The Delta

NEAP TIDE: *n. A weak tide that occurs near the quarter moon phase when the gravitational force of the sun and moon are perpendicular to each other with respect to the Earth.*

It was early June, the week before John and I would be going to far western Alaska, where he had secured summer jobs for us, working as field assistants on a bird research project. There were a few days' worth of work in Anchorage, sorting through and packing up equipment and buying gear, before we would fly out to the research camp. We drove north up the highway. Dirty piles of snow lingered near the road where small avalanches had bulldozed down and come to a halt. Rushing snowmelt whitened every drainage, but everything else was green.

We'd been hired by a biologist John had worked for during two summers while in college. We stayed in a back room at the biologist's house and spent our time driving from one side of Anchorage to the other, buying stuff John knew we needed for the field: hip waders, work pants, books and magazines. John and I considered the state's largest city not a destination but a place where we found ourselves out of necessity, usually on the way to somewhere else. Aside from visiting nearly every rubber boot outlet in Anchorage, we stuck tightly to our usual spots: the Asian market where we could find the curries and Thai spices not sold in Homer, a couple of giant thrift stores, a mediocre bagel joint, and the huge new and used book store.

Three days later, we boarded the flight from Anchorage to Bethel, which took a little over an hour. Heading west, the jet rose over the sharp peaks of the Alaska Range and the blue glaciers in between. Beyond the range's western foothills, the land flattened and stretched without interruption as far as I could see. John and I, along with two other biotechnicians, were the spike crew, the group that goes out early to get the project going before the ice flushed out of the rivers and the rest of the crew could arrive by boat. Susanna, a cheerful college student from the Midwest, made a third in our spike crew. Paul, a surly Gulf War veteran on his first trip to Alaska, appeared uninterested in everything around us.

We landed in late morning. Bethel's one-gate airport was crowded with Yup'ik families—reuniting happily, kissing, and calming babies. Some twenty-five thousand people, mostly Yup'ik, live in this community and the more than fifty small villages scattered along the region's many rivers. No roads lead here from the rest of the state. The service center for the region, Bethel is by far the largest community for hundreds of miles around, and has a runway that accommodates daily jets to and from Anchorage and a dock for cargo-bearing barges coming up the Kuskokwim from the Bering Sea. Uniformed white federal employees who worked for the vast national wildlife refuge surrounding Bethel moved decisively to gather gear and head out the door. Half a dozen men in clean camouflage getups milled about carrying fishing rod cases. They were on vacation and had spent a fortune to fly here and be taken to remote fishing camps. Many villagers didn't have cars—bringing them out by barge was prohibitively expensive—and taxis crowded the airport's curb.

As people milled by, moving duffels, plastic totes, and boxes, I stood at the edge of the curb and looked straight out ahead of me. From my vantage across this far edge of Bethel, the only signs of permanence were the power lines strung across the community and a few low houses that sat like paperweights on the tundra. I remembered how the land had looked on the maps at home—about as solid as cheese cloth. Except for unbroken, pale green strips on either sides of the rivers wide enough for the uppercase labels of "Yukon" and "Kuskokwim," the terrain had looked mysteriously gauzy, as if you could punch your fingers through the land and into the sea. And there was nothing beyond Bethel but small villages widely scattered across the tundra. Chakwaktolik, Nanvarnarluk, Tuluksak: the village names sang the stunted melodies of the Yup'ik language.

This was my first time off the road system in Alaska, and I was giddy. I was getting into a landscape with no limits and no easy passage to anywhere else. And the strange assemblage of people at the airport—the feds, the Natives, the tourists—meant there were many things about this place I didn't yet know. I stood in my stiff, new workpants; in six weeks they would be supple, even threadbare in places.

We were picked up by a man from a local floatplane company that would fly us the rest of the way to camp. He drove a diesel pickup with two rows of seats. Sixteen miles of gravel roads webbed through the flat, drab town, which was littered with the refuse of a windswept life. As we drove across Bethel to the company headquarters, we passed a hodgepodge of low-slung restaurants that revealed the remote community's surprising diversity: Mexican, Chinese, Albanian, Italian.

We loaded our gear into the back of a single-engine floatplane and took off from a wide eddy in the Kuskokwim River at the edge of town. While the pilot hummed to Jimmy Buffett singing through our headsets, one hundred miles of tundra rolled by beneath us, brown with a blush of early green and scattered scabs of snow. Rivers wound across the land inefficiently and between them, thousands of small, shallow lakes glinted like half-buried dimes. Below us, a few Native villages clumped messily on the land, radiating scars of four-wheeler and snowmachine tracks.

A lucky break in the traffic of truck-sized chunks of ice flushing out of the Manokinak River provided an opening for us to land on its wide, gray surface. The pilot watched for ice that could crumple his pontoons, and we quickly unloaded onto the muddy cut bank, where a couple of fuel barrels and a stack of grayed wood—anchored with rope and rebar stakes into the tundra—marked camp. As soon as the gear was out of the plane, the pilot jumped back into his seat, the engine roaring even before he had closed the door. For as far as we could see, nothing on the land rose higher than our knees. No trees, no shrubs, just watery mountains far in the distance. When the plane took off and was out of earshot, we were left only with a pile of gear, the vast dome of sky, and the wide river pushing ice out to the Bering Sea.

John took the lead in setting things up, mostly by just getting to work himself. We put up our sleeping tents and then a tent for gear, where we huddled to cook and eat dinner. Our field camp sat at the edge of the muddy Manokinak, which wandered slowly across a vast expanse of tundra. Half water, half earth, the region is dominated by two immense rivers, the Yukon and the Kuskokwim. The deltas of these rivers, which drain nearly half of the state, combine to form a flat, waterlogged landscape larger than the state of West Virginia. The region, called the Y-K Delta, is a wildly productive nursery for birds. Each summer, millions of waterfowl and shorebirds flock here to nest and raise young.

Once we had settled into camp, John trained us in how to get the project going. The goal of the research was to gather data about red-throated loons, duck-sized diving birds that nest in northern parts of North America, Europe, and Asia. The population of these birds in Alaska had dropped by half in less than twenty years and no one knew why. The Y-K Delta is the red-throated loons' most important nesting grounds in Alaska: More than a third of the population that nest in the state do so here, and this region had seen the most profound decline.

We began by working as a group of four, locating nests of our study species. In the spring, thousands of pairs of red-throated loons land on the Delta's shallow lakes and build nests along the shores. With legs set far back on their bodies, the birds are useless on land, so they assemble the wet mats of mud and vegetation that serve as their nests at the very edge of a lake. Their downy, gray chicks hatch in midsummer, and the parents feed them by mouth narrow silver fish that flash like blades. In the evenings, they wail out across the tundra.

We unpacked aerial photos that served as maps, and John showed us how to locate our position on the images by looking at the shapes of lakes, the curve of sloughs, and the minute changes in topography, and then how to carefully search for the nests and record the necessary data. Immersed once again in a world where John was teacher and I was student, I felt relieved when, once he showed us how to locate and record nests, we worked alone on the tundra, carrying a day's worth of food, water, and gear on our backs. Most days, the work wasn't difficult or exhausting, but engaging enough to make me forget about all the things I didn't know how to do around camp, such as build sturdy furniture out of the pile of wood or assemble the VHF antennae.

Before leaving camp in the morning, we put on heavy

rubber raincoats against the constant wind and hip waders to traverse the landscape, which was pocked by lakes and severed by sloughs. We fanned out into the tundra, scanning faraway lakes through binoculars, searching for the dark silhouettes of loons, with their characteristic upturned bills. The red-throats were skittish and flushed from their nests into the water long before we got close to them. As we approached, they would paddle nervously and then flap madly across the surface of a lake before flying away. We walked the rim of every lake carefully scanning for the loons' dinner plate–sized nests that held one or two chocolate-brown, speckled eggs. Most of these nameless lakes were smaller than swimming pools and no deeper than my thigh. Permafrost just a few feet beneath the ground kept them from getting any deeper. We waded out to every island, feeling the hardpan of frozen ground beneath our feet. On our plastic-coated photos, we marked every loon nest with a black dot and a code to distinguish it from every other nest we would find that summer. The work required little beyond the ability to walk long distances in hip waders and to locate yourself at a specific point in the midst of a landscape that looked nearly identical all around you, as well as a tendency to care about the project's success.

A WEEK LATER, a couple of hours past midnight, the sound of outboards drifted into my sleep like a mosquito in the ear. I awoke as John was leaving our tent. The rest of the crew arrived after a cold, six-hour trip on the river in two small skiffs and two wide aluminum boats. Five biologists, including the project director, were aboard the skiffs, which were heavy-laden with gear. The larger boats were run by four stocky Native herring fishermen who had broad, brown faces. They were hired to haul gear that couldn't fit in the small camp skiffs. These men lived in Chevak, a village of eight hundred people who spoke a unique dialect and called themselves *Cup'ik*. The skiffs we used all summer long were stored there between field seasons. Wearing every layer they had brought, topped off by sturdy rubber rain gear, the five biologists moved stiffly as we all gathered on the cut bank in the dusky light of the middle of the night to unload the boats. The Cup'ik men wore jeans, sweatshirts, light windbreakers, and baseball caps. The tide was out, and without much talk, we lugged dozens of heavy plastic totes from the boats onto the bank, now about ten feet above the river's surface. Four guys steadied themselves to heave the generator. With the engines cut, the night was quiet—even the birds were silent—but the banging of gear against the boats' hulls sounded like the striking of drums. The light was like that moment of dusk when trees rise as paper cuts against the sky. Here, that quality of light lingered.

I was curious about the new biotechs—these people I'd be living so closely with over the next few weeks. But more than that, I sought some kind of insight into the

men from Chevak, into how they lived, how they looked
at the Delta. They said little, just chuckling with each
other softly as they worked. John brought a pot of tea out
of the gear tent once the unpacking was done. We stood
on the bank of the river, in that extended twilight and
silently drank tea, holding the mugs with both hands so
as not to lose any warmth. One of the Cup'ik guys, who I
realized on closer glance was perhaps only fourteen, quietly broke the silence by telling us he had just written a
school report on a tundra plant called Labrador tea. "It's
got a lot of antioxidants," he said, that health magazine
term knocking around strangely in his mouth. Soon afterward, the Native men got back in their boats and took
off as the sky was beginning to get light.

Over the next few days, camp blossomed from a basic
shelter to a comfortable outpost. The project leader, Joel,
was in his late thirties and bumbled around camp in the
same pair of stained red sweatpants every day. He was
quiet but enjoyed the opportunity to laugh, and was
an easygoing boss. Field crews changed from season to
season, and the rest of our nine-person crew was a motley
assortment of college and graduate students in biology on
their summer break, and a volunteer in his sixties who
was less interested in work than in adding rare Eurasian
bird species to his life list.

We put up a weatherport, an uninsulated platform tent
tall enough to stand up in, which served as kitchen, living
room, and office. We furnished it with an oil heater, a

two-burner propane stove, folding chairs, shelves, and a kitchen table. One of the biotechs stapled a flowery plastic tablecloth to the table's ragged surface; spices, marinades, dry goods, canned food, and chocolate bars emerged from plastic totes.

Mornings at field camp normally passed leisurely. We packed into the weatherport, where the oil heater created the only warm, dry, and windless space for miles around. Unless someone decided to make pancakes for everyone or big omelettes from powdered eggs, we fended for ourselves, toasting bread on a cast-iron pan on the gas stovetop, passing around the drip coffee funnel, and rereading the dog-eared newsmagazines that had been sitting around the weatherport for a couple of weeks. Sometimes Joel relied on John, the only biotech in our group who had worked at this camp before, to help him plan the day's work at breakfast so we could all go off and do it on our own. After an hour or two of getting the morning going and packing lunch and gear, we departed on foot or by skiff for a day in the field.

But a week or so after the rest of the crew arrived, a wildlife vet flew into camp, igniting a buzz among the nine of us, and not just because he had brought a new crop of newspapers and magazines. The main goal of the season's research was to figure out where the region's population of red-throated loons spent the winter. The vet's job was to implant a satellite tracking device into the abdomens of a few red-throats. Provided everything worked correctly and the birds didn't die in the next few months, the implant would reveal where the birds migrated, which might yield a clue to why their numbers had declined so precipitously. That day, we were going to trap the first bird. Because Joel knew we all wanted to watch the surgery, he gave us this day "off," which meant we could linger around camp. We all knew that trapping and operating on these birds was risky. In previous cases, some wild birds reacted badly to the medication, abandoned their nests, or even died. With each individual bird seemingly important to the success of the entire species, the stakes were high and no one wanted to screw up.

At that point in the season, we each had a handful of nest dots on our maps. John had located one near camp, which gave us the first loon to trap that morning. We all trudged out to the tiny boomerang-shaped lake where we found the nest with one egg, the pair of red-throats long ago flushed and flown away. We watched from a tight circle while Joel unfolded the trap over the nest. It was a spring-loaded contraption about three feet in diameter, strung with cotton netting. He folded half of the trap back, against the push of the spring, and then kept the trap open with a stout nail threaded through the top of a plastic stake, which he hoped would hold in this waterlogged ground. Then he camouflaged the metal trap frame with sedge he tore up from the tundra around him. He unraveled string tied to the end of the nail which was wound on a kite spool, and then we all walked away from the nest, with the string unspooling behind us. We hoped the loons would return to the lake and the female would get back on the nest. Once she did, Joel would yank the string, triggering the trap to shut tight. Joel and one of the other biotechs waited behind a small mound for the birds to return; the rest of us walked back to the weatherport.

There was so much waiting involved in this work: waiting in the morning until the day's plan had been decided, waiting to find a loon nest among the dozens of goose, duck, and swan nests we passed as we worked. We waited out rainy days in the weatherport so that we wouldn't flush birds off their nests, exposing sensitive eggs to a cold rain, and we waited for each other, after a day surveying study plots downriver, to take the skiff together back to camp. But the disappearance of these birds brought a particular urgency to our work. So much basic information about them was unknown. No one knew their wintering grounds, what they ate, or what was causing their decline. And no one knew how much time might be left to figure it out. We felt we were working in the moment that would decide whether the red-throats survived or failed. And if they failed, one piece of the region would be lost, one species gone that was connected to all the other species in ways no one could ever fully grasp. One strand of the Delta's story would unravel: A Yup'ik tale tells of two loons helping a blind man regain sight.

MUCH ABOUT THE life here was similar to what I had come to learn back home, but the Delta had its own parameters. Tides weren't nearly as extreme here as in Homer, but you had to keep track of them, because a slough that cut a deep channel into your study plot might be a narrow trickle to cross at low tide, but would be a very cold swim when the water level rose almost a dozen feet later in the day and you wanted to get back to camp. I learned that running boats was a different thing in this muddy landscape than back home, where in the bay you had to be alert for submerged rocks. There were no rocks here, but the gray water masked mudflats that could trap even the most experienced boater. So you drove the skiff along the side of the river with the steep cut bank where the water was deeper, rather than closer to gently sloping mudflats. John gave me a lesson on a camp skiff one evening on the river, but when I accidentally opened the throttle when I meant to slow down, I vowed not to drive the boats anymore, and instead to sit in the bow and look out at the open country moving by.

On the Delta, land was a tenuous seam binding sea and sky. A pile of dust scraped off inland mountains and splayed out by the rivers, the region was shifty and nothing was solid. Hundreds of rivers migrated across the tundra, carving new curves, shrugging off old ones, and dropping deep, slippery mud where they slowed. On an incoming tide, the Bering Sea fingered into tidal sloughs, overtaking the flat land with its fragrance, and carting off with earth when it left. Each summer, I learned, camp was moved back a dozen feet, as the river gnawed away at its bank.

As soon as the snow broke into patches in spring, the Delta was thick with birds. Within a week of arriving, I had become familiar with the nearly three dozen species that nested around camp as if they were neighbors. The diversity spanned dainty songbirds to long-legged shorebirds, more than a dozen species of ducks and geese, raptors, cranes, and unwieldy swans. John helped me see the differences between all of the shorebirds—some of which I recognized from the thick flocks that stopped over at our bay back home. And he helped me hear the varied music of these birds: Savannah sparrows called in trills, black-bellied plovers sang from the highlands up-river, and willow ptarmigans burst with throaty laughs. The tundra extended as far as we could see, and each step revealed a vast thickness of birds. As we walked across our research plots, we parted flocks of brant geese whose prim black and white plumage made them look like a crowd of white-collar commuters waiting for the morning train. Inadvertently, we flushed countless shorebirds from their expertly concealed nests and scared mother geese into hunkering low on their nests. And a dunlin, a robin-sized shorebird with a black patch on its belly, perched atop our tent in the evenings and sang into the night.

While birds dominated the soggy landscape, Arctic foxes slunk by from time to time sniffing out a meal, and mouse-sized voles streaked occasionally across the weatherport floor. But it seemed as if the birds, with their deliberately engineered nests, their careful tracks across the mud, were the only things that kept the Delta from washing completely away.


I HAD SPENT a few summers on a trail crew and I loved living and working outside once again. I got used to the rhythm of chores: making dinner for everyone after a day in the field if you were among the first ones back to camp; hauling wash water in buckets from a nearby lake, brackish because it got inundated a few times a year by extremely high tides and swimming with tiny gray invertebrates. We took turns washing dishes after dinner at a table at the edge of the river, looking north as the sky turned pink. At that time of evening, loons flew downriver out to sea to feed, quacking loudly over our heads. It was the only time we used warm water for washing— heated on the propane stove—and as I soaked my hands, the dishwater melted away the chapping from wind and sun and the crescent moons of dirt beneath my fingernails. Our outhouse was a plywood shack standing at the edge of the river about a hundred yards from camp with a plastic toilet seat perched atop a five-gallon plastic bucket. Dumping the bucket in the river was a hated chore. When it wasn't storming, I washed myself at the end of the day by dunking in the frigid wash water lake, where my toes sank deep into muck. As a pair of Arctic terns nesting on the lake dove at my head, I stood naked on the tundra to shampoo and soap up before dunking once more. I had never felt so clean in my life.

Even though I had the familiar sense of life paring down to its most important components—eat, work, wash, sleep—there was much that surprised me about life on the Delta. The day the tree swallows showed up in camp, I was shocked by the covetousness that possessed me in the midst of this communal life where possessions—a good novel, sunscreen, a bottle of Glenlivet—were few and easily shared. I wanted to keep the birds around, to have them nest here and be our pets. These brilliant blue-green birds nest in tree cavities, and we watched the four birds flit around camp exploring every possible nesting site: the vacant circle in the battered weatherport door where a doorknob should have been, a hole in the metal cap on the top of a propane tank. We were surrounded by nesting birds, but that morning, nothing seemed more important than keeping the swallows at this stop on their migration farther north, where they would find trees. A couple of the other biotechs and I ran around camp looking for supplies to make a nesting box. We sloppily hammered together a few pieces of wood, knocked out a knot to create a perfect swallow-sized hole, and then attached the wooden box with duct tape to a metal pole pounded into the tundra. We waited. One swallow landed on the box and inspected it. I held my breath. Unsuitable. In a few minutes, they were gone.

I was surprised, too, by the feeling that, although we all meant well and cared about the birds, just by being out here we were doing harm. As we walked across our plots, we flushed all kinds of birds from their nests, and sometimes gulls would fly in to take advantage of the unprotected eggs for a meal. Foxes scampered across the tundra and we suspected that they might be following our scents from nest to nest so they, too, could find easy food.

I had tried to prepare myself to once more be on John's turf. But the more I depended on him to be my teacher, the more I shied away from him in every other way. So after dinner, I went to the tent and wrote in my journal to be alone. I described the varieties of mud—the deep stuff that had swallowed one of the other women's hip waders one afternoon, setting us off into fits of laughter, and the drier mud, broken into continent-shaped fragments, which made the ground look like a gathering of maps. I recorded the strict hierarchy of water: the river, which was our road and drain; the wash water lake we returned to daily; and the blue plastic barrels of drinking water that had been hauled to camp by snowmachine in early spring by a couple of men from Chevak. I recorded small things I saw around me: a cold addled egg kicked out of a white-fronted goose's nest; a dead shorebird stiff on the tundra; and groups of male common eiders in handsome black-and-white plumage with green on the backs of their heads who had left their mates to care for the eggs and hatchlings for the rest of the summer. Getting these sights down on paper became my own project.

I QUICKLY BECAME sensitive to the Delta's subtle beauty. Nothing was showy about its stark horizon nor the plants that hugged this windswept land. The gray rivers were slow and flat. There were no dangerous large mammals around. A layer of fine mud coated everything so that when the veterinarian arrived—stepping out of the plane in clean jeans and loafers—he sparkled, everything metallic and unmuddied on him flashing: his watch, his wedding ring, the frames of his glasses. There was, however, nothing subtle about the turn of this season. It was the fastest, fiercest summer I'd ever known—flaring the tundra from brown to green in a matter of days, erupting with hatching birds, and illuminated by constant sun. Months of dark cold kept the Delta silent; now its real self emerged: plain, radiant, full of life.

In comparison to the Delta, Homer was a cluttered mess. Back home, electric lines intersected rooftops, roads crisscrossed creeks, and street signs pointed all over town. Having come to love a place bound by coastline and bluff, where the sky was interrupted by mountains and ragged stands of spruce, I was surprised at how fiercely I was drawn to the Delta's clean divisions between river, bank, sky. An ancient landscape, the Delta was formed by the sloughing away of old mountains, yet the land renewed itself continually, refreshed with every influx of tide, scraped clean by the constancy of rivers. There was nearly continuous cacophony—the metallic melodies of Lapland longspurs, the coughing of tundra swans as they flew overhead, the barking of geese, the wailing and wailing of loons. Yet I had never known such silence.

I was entranced by the emptiness, the lack of human-made boundaries. At once a big empty bed just made up with fresh sheets and a blank page, the Delta's flawless plain calmed and invigorated me. In rubber raincoat and boots, I lay in an $X$ on the tundra, the vectors of my limbs shooting out infinitely. This was what it feels like to be cocooned by open space.

Often in the middle of the day I took a lunch break on one of the large pieces of driftwood that had washed downriver and been dropped far inland by the spring and fall high tides. Stripped of bark and washed smooth by months or years of sea and weather, the wood provided a dry place to sit with my back to the wind and pull out lunch from my pack. These pieces of driftwood were the largest things on the tundra, and with no other objects competing on the horizon, they loomed in the distance. Many were marked by an axe's notch, signaling that they had been claimed by Native villagers and would be collected in winter when the Delta was frozen, when ice bridged the rivers and the terrain was easily navigable by snowmachine. Traditionally, the Yup'ik had used driftwood posts to support their semiburied sod homes and had stretched skins across driftwood frames for boats. Modern villagers lived in stick frame or prefabricated houses and owned skiffs with outboard engines; but in this treeless, shifty landscape, wood was still essential for sauna fires and to make racks for drying fish.

For enough years to witness the great movements of rivers, Yup'ik people relied on the Delta's resources, living off its fish and seals, berries and whales, the heat of sweatbaths and the spotless cold of winter. The Internet had come to Delta villages, and while digital delivery of the rest of the world was speeding up every year, subsistence was a way of life among most Yup'ik here, and schools taught classes in the Native language. In summer, cut banks near the villages were dotted with fish camps, where families combed salmon out of muddy rivers with wide gill nets and dried them on wooden racks. Fishermen pulled bottom-dwelling fish up with longlines and took freshwater fish with handheld nets. Yup'ik families fanned out into the tundra to harvest berries and gathered at the mouths of rivers to shoot seals. As the days shortened, hunters traveled upriver for moose and caribou and hooked fish through holes in the ice. After a winter of eating their stores of dried meat and fish, the villages celebrated spring as the start of the new season of fresh, wild food. The Yup'ik name for April means "bird place," and the arrival of millions of birds meant an abundance of things to eat.

You could call this the most remote region in the country. We were five hundred miles off the road system, in a region uninhabited for many miles. I loved being so far from communication; we were far from phone lines and the reach of the Internet, and had only a VHF radio to talk to other research camps and passing pilots as well as a suitcase-sized satellite phone for emergencies. There wouldn't even be a way to send a letter once the vet flew out in a day or so. Still, evidence of the rest of the world was scattered everywhere. I found spent shotgun shells on the tundra, a plastic drink bottle from China, and a beautiful blue glass globe the size of an orange—a float from a Japanese fishing net. And this seemingly limitless landscape was not without limitations. Federal regulators restricted hunting on the Delta because of declining bird populations, limiting even subsistence harvests. Home, pantry, woodshed to a subsistence lifestyle, the Delta— much of it protected as the Yukon Delta National Wildlife Refuge—was otherwise useless to the cash economy: not yet determined to be particularly valuable for mining, oil and gas development, or extended residential settlement. The Delta's soggy landscape was similar to the Arctic refuge's flat, bird-flecked tundra; but its uselessness was as yet its savior, and the Delta went largely unnoticed.

A LITTLE OVER an hour after Joel had set the trap on the loon's nest, he rushed in the weatherport door with the bird in a plastic pet carrier. Joel and the vet then went quickly to work. Joel took the loon out of the carrier and held the bird on the kitchen table, pinning its wings down under his hands. The loon looked terrified: its red eyes flared and its black bill darted at the vet like a dagger. Joel took it under one hand and used the other to still its head. The loon pushed its webbed feet madly against the flowered plastic tablecloth until the vet injected anesthesia into its leg and within a few seconds, the bird's feet stilled and its head began to wobble. Then the loon went completely limp and its bill lay on its breast. The vet laid the animal—which at that point looked like a carcass—on a clean cloth on the kitchen table and inserted a tube into its mouth. The tube connected to a soft bulb that Joel pumped to deliver air into the loon's lungs.

Crowding the weatherport, we were all silent except for the few words exchanged between Joel and the vet. I was transfixed by how dead the bird looked, and how the vet seemed to keep this bird just above death. Lifeless, it had dulled. The pale gray of its head, which normally shimmered, lost its luster, and the darker gray of its neck, which was made up of fine, pinstriped feathers, looked messy. From a distance, through binoculars, these birds always looked perfect; they shone. Now it lay ringed by the tools and trash of our work: bottles, tubes, needles, blades, iodine-soaked cloths, and a beeping heart monitor.

Then the vet began the work of inserting the matchbox-sized transmitter into the bird's lower back. He parted the feathers to make an incision. I looked away then, feeling my head starting to swirl and sweat breaking out across my body. The bird suddenly flapped, surprising all of us, and the vet quickly delivered more anesthesia through the syringe attached to its leg. He inserted the transmitter into a sterile gauze pouch and then worked it into the animal's body through the incision. I felt ill, easily sickened by the gore, but also lightheaded at the control we had over this bird, how easily we could take its life in our hands and splay it out on our kitchen table. I knew I was weak, but I had to dash out of the weatherport and sit outside with my head between my knees until the nausea subsided.

The whole business seemed so cruel, but Joel had assured us that only a few birds needed to be outfitted with the transmitters in order to get useful data about the species. Gathering basic information about these birds was a necessary first step. But then what? Would a culprit ever be found? Could a cause of their decline be proven? Would action be taken? What if—as Joel wondered—these birds weren't getting enough food to thrive and feed their young because the Bering Sea was changing? Then what? What changes could be made fast enough to make a difference?

WHEN THE PROCEDURE was completed, the vet put the limp bird—which now had a six-inch-long, black rubberized antenna sticking out of her back—into the pet carrier and Joel brought it outside to a quiet spot in camp and put a tarp over it. We waited for the bird to regain consciousness, and then Joel carried the kennel and we all walked back to the boomerang lake, empty of the loon's mate. He put the carrier down next to the nest, opened the door, and pulled out the bird, setting it down beside the nest. Still groggy, she stared out at us with red eyes atop a wobbling head. The antenna stuck alertly into the air.

"Let's go," Joel said. We all retreated quickly from the nest and walked toward camp. We stopped from time to time, checking the bird through binoculars. The loon had already slid into the small lake and was paddling around with her wings flapping uselessly.

In the coming months and years, the research would progress slowly. The transmitters revealed that the population of red-throated loons nesting on the Delta migrated down the West Coast of North America as far south as California. This information provided a critical clue, but it didn't solve anything; it was a tiny prelude to the rest of a story whose end no one could predict.

A few weeks later, John and I headed home. On the flight out, as I looked from the floatplane for swan families on lakes, I realized that despite everything I couldn't do and didn't know, I felt adept as a witness to the Delta, which was in the midst of changes far beyond what the few research camps scattered across the region could measure. The calculations of cause were so complex. I dwelled in what I could see and record: a cache of ping-pong ball–like eggs under a piece of driftwood that was a short-eared owl's nest; the white heads of emperor geese stained gold by iron in the mud; the way camp shrank from black dots on the horizon to nothing as I worked my way across the tundra. At home, I put the blue glass globe from the Japanese fishing net on the windowsill, where it gathered light. It was a token smuggled from another world, borrowed by me for a time. It was a reminder that a domain once claimed can be lost.

# 11

# Staking Claim

STEVEDORE: *n. One who is employed in the loading or unloading of ships. v. To load or unload the cargo of a ship.*

The property was perfect. It was six acres that abutted eighty acres of scattered spruce forest that were protected by law for moose habitat. A meadow ran across it, north to south, draped with grasses and thick with the fuchsia flowers of chest-high fireweed. At the far end of the meadow, the snow-capped peaks of the mountains across the bay rose up above the black tips of spruce. A stream slipped along the edge of the meadow. Running water on the property: This felt like a dream. There was nothing between the southern edge of the land and the bluff down to the beach except a mile and a half of spruce, the slice of Fritz Creek—as wide as a rural lane—and the kind of boggy habitat where we hoped wild cranberries grew. Standing on the property, you couldn't hear the road. It was seven miles out of town to the east, in a microclimate that was generally warmer in the summer and colder in the winter than town. We liked that. It meant

perfect gardening conditions—for the north, at least—
and in winter, we'd get snow when town was getting rain.
And the meadow collected sun for many hours during
the summer days; we could tell this even at the end of
August when we found the place and bought it.

The property had no water view. This was perfect too,
we thought. It made the land much cheaper—less than
some people paid for a new car. But just knowing that
there were no houses, no roads, no telephone or electric
lines between our place and the bay made us very happy.

We knew already which birds would pass through the
place. In the fall, we would hear great horned owls and see
hawk owls perched at the tops of our spruce. On winter
days, we knew that chickadees would buzz through in
small groups and dull red pine grosbeaks would gather in
the trees. In the spring, we'd awaken to hermit thrushes
and the three-note calls of golden-crowned sparrows and
fall asleep to robins' songs that would play long into the
night. In the summer, kinglets would sing incessantly
and cranes would fly overhead, sounding their rattle-like
calls as they passed. We would hang a feeder from a tall
birch with a perfectly placed bough and keep it filled all
year long.

The land had beautiful trees. Birches lined the gravel
driveway that curved a quarter-mile into the property.
Their boughs spread like arms infinitely fingered. I loved
the jagged edges and strong venation of birch leaves and
the way that whole canopies lit yellow with the first deep
frosts of fall. We had plenty of spruce, both live and those

killed by bark beetles. There were enough dead spruce to bring down for ample supplies of firewood. Thick alders masked the view of neighbors, making the place feel private and wild. Nearby, along the creek, tall cottonwoods grew in pairs. In late summer, they would cast off minute seeds in downy nebulae that would zoom across our acres. And in the spring, scrubby willows would reach pawlike flowers over the banks of the creek.

The night after John and I signed on the property, we stayed up long past the sun had gone down talking incessantly about our plans. We would turn the unfinished, two-story structure that sat next to the driveway into a workshop, with a little apartment above it for visitors, or a renter, even. We would turn the earth over and grow a large garden. We would have chickens. We would ski from the property in the winter, and walk along the creek in the summer, and take cold dips in it. We would build a sauna and fill buckets with water from the creek to throw over our heads.

The weekend after buying the place, we set out to explore. From the end of the meadow, we walked south, toward the bay. Damp grasses licked our rubber boots until they shone. We examined the small stream for aquatic insects and found none, though I was certain we'd see them in the spring. We crossed Fritz Creek, which was one of the largest that ran off the bluff into the bay, on the back of a fallen cottonwood, and spotted a pair of harlequin ducks from the far bank. These shy birds were John's darlings. The male had plumage as playfully colored as a court jester—bold white markings on a blue head, with red crown and flanks. This species of sea duck nests along remote freshwater creeks and rivers in the summer. We were thrilled. Maybe we'd have our own nesting pair nearby.

Farther along, at the edge of a pillowy upland area covered in crowberries, squat spruce, and a miniature form of birch, we came across a small clearing where the ground had been torn up. We found moose hairs, then part of a bloodied backbone. We circled the bear kill cautiously—irresistibly curious about the attack yet knowing that the bear could still be nearby. Then we saw the skull—cleaned of skin and blood: It belonged to one of this year's calves. We loved knowing there were bears nearby and that they hunted not far from our new place, that we would be able to witness these other lives. All of this, too, seemed perfect.

But we couldn't move in yet. There wasn't a place to live, and the property needed work. A forty-foot-long dilapidated trailer house stretched across the end of the driveway. The previous owners had parked it there twenty years ago. Its aluminum siding—white with a pale blue trim—was falling down. Inside, it was a mess. It looked as though the previous owners had just up and left one afternoon and never returned. A coffee mug sat on the counter and cans of food crowded the cupboards. The bedroom was littered with clothes and children's books with curled pages. The place was unlivable. The carpet had gone moldy and bad. The walls sagged. The countertop was peeling off. The place stank of the rot of manmade things. But John and I weren't fazed. We would get rid of it. John assured me we could hire someone to haul it to the dump, where it could be gotten rid of for free. We would clean up the mess. We would take down a sloppy shed that had been added onto the trailer. John looked at a tiny one-room cabin that had been built behind the trailer—presumably as an extra bedroom—and knew immediately that we could convert it into a place where we could live. We would add on to it and make it ours.

There was other work to be done. The property was littered with other remnants of the previous owners. Dozens of crab pots—with a diameter the size of eighteen-wheeler tires—were stacked along the driveway. An old truck—with four flat tires—had been pushed off the driveway and sat nosed up into a stand of spruce. Boat parts—an anchor, an engine, the mold of a hull—sat in thick grass. There were rusty drums and old boat batteries parked along the driveway, and wooden pallets that had been tossed haphazardly everywhere. A skeet shooter stood on a spruce pole platform in the grass, and we found clay pigeons scattered across the meadow. A chicken coop built with spruce siding and the frame of a greenhouse were falling apart on either side of the meadow. And there was so much other junk. But when I cupped my hands on either side of my face—to block out the decrepit trailer, the glassless greenhouse, the rotting chicken coop—what I saw was the long grassy meadow edged by spruce, the peaks of the mountains across the bay, and our own slice of sky.

SINCE MOVING TO Alaska, we had been surrounded by people who had bought land and built their own homes. There were Dave and Rebecca, whose property, farther out of town than ours, dipped to the southeast, granting them a view of the head of the bay and up a glacier-filled valley on the south shore. They had put up a small, two-story place and kept adding on as their family grew. They had a chicken coop—made out of an old wooden boat— and their toilet was a five-gallon bucket they emptied onto a compost pile in the yard. I couldn't imagine what Rebecca's parents thought when they came up to visit from their retirement home in Florida. Another friend, Sasha, had bought eight acres thirteen miles out of town that had a small cabin on it. When Collin came into her life, they got pigs and another dog, extended the garden, and started building a workshop. It seemed everyone was in some stage of buying land or building. And it seemed that this is what everyone did who stayed: They staked out their own piece of land, then made it theirs. They cleared and built, graded and maintained.

For a year, John had been suggesting that we buy a place. But I had resisted. I wasn't ready for the responsibilities or the commitment. At the back of my mind, I always wondered if I'd return to the East. But I had been romanced: by the way pairs of ravens tangoed across the sky; by moose tracks left provocatively along streets in the middle of town; by the musk of the sea. And the month on the Delta left me swooning. This was a rich life. I loved the way hills unrolled endlessly behind town, and how, at the foot of them sat a strip of undeveloped beach. Undeveloped beach—where else could you find that? Here, streams ran unfettered to the sea. Migratory birds flew in and out unimpeded. Moose dropped calves around town. As each year passed, the seasons changed how I lived. I knew the species of trees and the low plants that grew in the taiga, in meadows, along the trails in the dense woods across the bay. I was beginning to be able to identify every bird I saw. I knew where to find clams and mussels, and was learning the names of the creeks that veined down the bluff behind town and made their way to the beach. I could gather up my courage to paddle across the bay; I could fill my boat with fish. I knew the names of many of the fjords and inlets created by the furrowed coastline on the south side of the bay: Tutka, China Poot, Peterson, Sadie. This, to me, was what home meant. And so, three years after moving here, I woke up one Saturday and told John it was time to look for a place.

Here, buying property wasn't just about buying a place to live; it was often about buying a place to *produce*, to support yourself. We wanted to grow food, collect eggs from a coop full of hens. We wanted to heat our house for free and use water from the creek to douse veggies in the garden.

During the weeks after our purchase, we walked the property to find its corners, which were marked with pink plastic tape. We made plans about how to proceed. John had ideas about how everything should be done: how the trailer should be moved, a cabin built around the existing structure, the place cleaned up. On our days off, we left our rental place in the morning to drive out to the property and didn't return until dinnertime. We hacked down outbuildings and threw the wood onto a swelling burn pile. John climbed onto the top of the shed and removed the aluminum roofing. We set it aside to use for the cabin. For days I moved junk from one end of the property to the other. There were buckets of damp nails, old tools unusable because of rust, tangles and tangles of line. With everything, we made the decision: keep it, burn it, or take it to the dump. We spent days dismantling, burning, setting aside, and cleaning up. Still, there was no end in sight.

During these weeks, we scanned maps, seeing how the outline of our property fit into the land around it: the winding course of the creek, the route we could take to walk to a nearby lake no roads led to, the land protected from development, future subdivisions, neighbors' parcels. We were so proud of our rectangle and the way it shared a boundary with land that would forever be free from roads, houses, strip malls.

All around our property, signs of ownership had been stamped onto the land. Homesteaders and early settlers had left their names on nearby roads: Thurston, Waterman, Kilcher, Greer. And across the map of the entire state, names reflected other kinds of ownership. The Russian: Bobrof Island, Mount Sergief, Strogonof Point, and Pavlof Volcano. The Native: Aiautak Lagoon, Kinipaghalghat Mountains, Takrak River, Hochandochtla Peak, and Kalakaket Creek. The British: Cook Inlet, Prince of Wales Island, Prince William Sound, and Bristol Bay.

Naming was one of the many ways to try to own a place. For our six acres, you wrote out a check and signed your name on a stack of papers at an office on one side of town. When the papers were filed at an office on the other side of town, ownership was official. Natives had owned the region by living here, by eating of the place, by surviving. Russians had doled out charters to companies; these pieces of paper granted them rights to natural resources, which they often took by force. Homesteaders filed a claim, paid a fee, lived on their allotment for five years, built a home, and farmed the land. Then they could "prove up" and the land was theirs. Not far up the highway you could turn off it, drive another thirty-five miles, and hike on the beach to a promontory of land that looks across the water to Anchorage. Here, at Point Possession, in 1778, after failing to find the fabled Northwest Passage, Captain Cook sent one of his men ashore to bury a brandy bottle containing a parchment that claimed all of the surrounding lands for England. Today, this tip of land remains testament to how so many acts of ownership mean nothing.

ONE WEEKEND, AT the end of a day of work on the land, we stopped by the house of a couple I knew who lived on the road: Rick and Lauren. He was tall and soft-spoken, like John, but with a long ponytail of nearly black hair falling down his back. She was a bookworm from Montreal with a sharp wit that reminded me of people I knew back East. They weren't back-to-the-landers. They were professionals who worked in town and were talking about leaving the state for graduate school. "You'll need a French drain," Lauren instructed. This was a fancy term for a ditch that would divert water away from the house. "It'll keep your place from becoming a pile of mud in the spring." She laughed. John and I looked at each other. "We know someone with a Bobcat," Lauren said quickly. "I can give you his number."

Other neighbors walked up the driveway one afternoon and introduced themselves as we were throwing junk onto the burn pile. They were a couple in their fifties, both tall, with short, graying hair. "Why don't you come over for dinner tonight?" they asked. So we did. When it got too dark to work, we drove up the road a couple of miles to pick up a bottle of wine, then came back, parked at the property, and walked over. They were drunk by the time we got there. Over pan-fried T-bones and more wine, they slurred about how badly they wanted to leave the state. Their grown daughter back East, the long winters, the too-small town. They had nailed a FOR SALE BY OWNER sign onto the trunk of a birch at the end of their driveway, which was the last place on the road. They hoped they weren't asking too much.

Weeks later, when John was at the property alone, a pair of Mormon missionaries hiked up the driveway in their blacks and whites. You could spot the traveling Mormons from a mile away: They were the only men in town who wore suits. And their hair was neatly trimmed, their faces clean-shaven, and their shoes made for pavement. "I wanted to offer them tea," John reported to me later. "But I didn't have a stove or a pot. So instead, I asked them to leave."

We were in the middle of sorting through old fishing gear piled beneath the two-story shed one afternoon when we heard a high-pitched shriek coming from someplace beyond the bottom of the driveway. It continued, like the sound of a pained question, the tone rising at the end. It was somehow familiar, but I couldn't place it. John didn't know either. We walked to the road where a man with a skinny, gray braid hanging down his neck and a cigarette between his fingers stood looking up into a tall spruce. He lived up the road. "Bear cubs," he said. "Must have lost their mama. Just called Fish and Game. They're sending someone out." As we stood there, the sound continued and a scene flashed through my head of a long-past summer in the Rockies that I'd spent clearing trails, when I'd seen some small dark animal up a tree, a dark shape with spines. "Sounds kind of like a porcupine," I mumbled. "Naw. Just some lost bear cubs crying for their mama," the man said.

A mint green Fish and Game truck came down the road and stopped near us, the engine idling. The driver rolled down the window. "Hey Bill," he said to the man with the braid. "Howdy," he said to us. He listened for a minute to the shrieks. "What you got there is a porcupine. And we'll just leave him be," the Fish and Game man said before turning his truck around and taking off. For a moment, I felt the small victory of having had the answer to that high-pitched question. I so badly wanted to have that answer, to have any answers.

As fall ticked by and winter's dark sky began to hang lower and closer, the days we spent working on the property felt long and damp. The leaves dropped and the grasses died back, shoving into the fore all the work we hadn't done: the broken wood pallets we hadn't burned, the deflated buoys we hadn't taken to the dump, the defunct truck we hadn't towed away. But our dreams kept the despair at bay: We talked about the seeds we would plant in the spring, the ski routes we wanted to explore from the place that winter, the colors we would paint the walls and plywood floor of the cabin.

Every weekend, we worked all day then fell into bed exhausted, the smell of the burnpile lingering in our hair and in the heap of clothes we'd stripped off in the corner of the room. Pretty soon we realized the two-story building would have to be torn down—the stairs swayed beneath our feet and the pressboard floor had rotten out. We realized the previous owner never would come pick up the crab pots, car batteries, and fifty-five-gallon drums as he'd promised. We realized we would spend years pulling nails out of the soles of our shoes.

But John worked on, decisive and undeterred. Part of me wanted to torch everything, the other part wanted to examine it all as if sorting through an ancient midden. What clues did this junk provide? What could we save to use again? My uncertainty bred deliberation; the deliberation bred inefficiency. While I debated what was useful and what was junk, John dismantled sheds, hired a man to tow the trailer away, rigged up an outhouse. He kept one eye perpetually scanning for deals, for tools, for things we would need on our land. As the days passed, his vision of the place came into sharp focus, yet mine began to waver.

As John labored on optimistically, I began to doubt whether I could hack it. The amount of work we put in didn't translate readily into results. The cabin no longer seemed like our perfect homestead, but a dark, close space. As we nailed down tongue and groove spruce flooring in the sleeping loft, I stopped being able to picture myself lying on the futon there next to John. Instead of the property making me feel closer to him, I felt acres apart.

After a weekend spent in my grubbiest clothes, I started wearing lipstick to work during the week. That fall, my skin turned colorless like the terrain outside—washed out, as fall always was. On the weekends, I strained to imagine how John and I would fix up the cabin—where a small fridge and a wood stove would go; how we'd build kitchen countertops and shelves; how we'd rig up a simple bath; what we'd plant in garden beds next to the house. Come Monday, I marked the movements through my office window of the yellow truck owned by a shy crab fisherman I barely knew. Somewhere along there—in the muddle of pry bars, rusty nails, the smell of old fiberglass insulation, rotting spruce posts, and sinkholes in the yard that we thought might hold twenty-year-old sewage— part of me had wandered off.

Figuring out—and fixing—what's broken is so much harder than building anew. At the ready we had level, chalk line, and square. Our measurements were clean and we knew that as the ground shifted beneath the skids on which the cabin sat, we would have to shim the corners to make it right. But I had no shims to prop up myself. Despite our six acres, and the neighboring eighty we believed the moose would willingly share, the boundary of our ownership became a string of impossibilities to me: impossible to have the freedom I wanted, the space I craved. I felt monstrously cruel and couldn't find the words to describe what was wrong: *I want my own desk* was all I could manage to say. In the two-room cabin we'd devised, there wasn't space.

I wanted to freeze time. I wanted to stop the mushrooming of our to-do list out on the property. I thought if the clock paused, I could make sense of everything. Instead, winter smothered fall and one night, huddled near the heater at our rental place, the words were choking me. *I need to go.* John went in to the bathroom and closed the door. When he came out, he lay on the bed. I wanted to lie down next to him; we were each other's comfort.

"Please leave," he said.

Four years had whittled down to this: Words stuck in the throat. A desire to cling to the very thing I was running from. An inability to say what I really felt, because I didn't yet know how to describe it. I had hurt John beyond measure and I hated myself for it. But a quiet wave of relief washed over me.

In the weeks that followed, I emptied our place of my things. It wasn't hard to figure out which stuff belonged to me; I realized in my mind, my things had remained separate all along. My old red station wagon proved a second home; it could carry everything I needed and it always started up. Friends helped carry my piano across the snow. I hadn't realized that, called to provide a little muscle, they'd witness this unraveling. I didn't want to see them again for a while. In the winter air, the instrument's soundboard shrank. But it kept tune enough. I clung to the keyboard, to Chopin nocturnes, Bach preludes, and those ponderously melodic pieces of Russian Romantics. Now there was something immensely practical in the lacy scores that had gathered dust for months.

FOR A LITTLE while, I'd had what I thought I'd always wanted: a little piece of Alaska. But that January, I took off. This was a tenet of the modern back-to-the-land lifestyle: You could abandon it. The land, the project had been a choice. I realized I was done with it: the sense of idleness I felt next to John's industry, a partnership that had squandered passion for practicality, months spent sorting through the jetsam of others' lives. I moved alone to a place on the beach where the constant flux of tides felt reassuring.

# 12

# POSSESSION

DEAD RECKONING: *n. The process of determining the position of a vessel at any instant by applying to the last well-determined position the run that has since been made.*

The small house perched at the edge of the bay was just what I needed. It was a few miles out of town, distanced from passing cars by a field of spruce stumps and elderberry shrubs. I didn't know the neighbors.

The house belonged to an older woman I knew through a class I'd taken at the college. She had left town to spend the winter in Arizona, where she was seeking treatment for debilitating arthritis. I had tracked her down by phone and mumbled into the receiver something about "going through a hard time." "Can I stay in your place for a little while?" I asked. There was a pause. "Okay," she said. "Just pay the heating bill."

I got keys from a neighbor and brought a carload of boxes and bags to the house. I swept a small upstairs room clean of dead flies and spread out my things. As I unpacked my books, I remembered the way I had looked at these same books sandwiched together with John's on our shelves. His library of reference books—on natural history, home building, geography—were the kinds of resources one needed, I had thought, to live in and understand the world. At the time, my volumes seemed only to prove something lacking in me, my inability to store and use important information. But wedged together on this small, empty shelf, the books formed an odd assemblage that traced my history—novels that had taken me into worlds I wanted to keep within arm's reach, books that had been gifts over the years from people I loved, an assortment of poetry volumes I turned to from time to time.

Because of her arthritis, the woman who owned the place had been confined to the downstairs. Friends had wheeled a hospital bed into the middle of the living room. And as she was a widow and had no one around to remind her, she left messages to herself on yellow sticky notes posted around the house: "Think of 10 good things that happened today." "Smile." "Don't strain your wrist— hold phone loosely."

That winter was a cold one. A blue-white skin of ice formed on the surface of the bay in a small inlet protected by the Spit. The kitchen windows looked out onto the bay, and the shape-shifting ice was mesmerizing. The tide floated sheets of ice close to shore and then dropped them onto the frozen mudflats. The ice rolled and pulsed above the water and split and heaved as the bay changed shape. The ice could look blue, or white, or gray; it could seem solid or liquid, like great planes or millions of shards. The sea was a welcome distraction.

At night, however, when the windows turned to mirrors, they threw reflections at me. I saw how my small breasts had started drooping and how my cotton underwear sagged. I saw how winter dulled the blond streaks that summer had laid in my hair and I recognized the angles I'd never liked in my face. It was impossible to look away.

Almost daily, I walked out the back door down the snow-covered trail that crisscrossed the slope down to the beach. Along the edges of the trail, dry branches of wild roses punctured the snow and offered shriveled, rust-colored hips. On the beach, I pushed my rubber boots through dry salt slush at the edge of the water. On these cold days, the receding tide glazed over the cobble beach in ice. As I walked along the beach, I tried to see everything I thought John would see on a walk like this: the raft of scoters out on the open water, the direction of the wind and what that might mean for tomorrow's weather, the ferry that arrived only on Tuesdays. Without John's keen eyes, however, I felt I never could see enough. Doubts perched in the periphery of my vision and squawked at me. I called friends, family, past boyfriends. I felt as though my motor had stalled and I was drifting toward the Inlet on an outgoing tide.

Leaving a man you love, a best friend, feels irrational. There is no way to think your way out of it. So I read novels that sucked me in while dozens of crows gathered on the metal roof above my bed. I left the television on for hours, the radio on after that. I shuddered at the thought of the pain I'd caused John. I knew it was harder to be left than to leave.

Through the kitchen window, I watched sea otters on the ice. Whenever I saw these animals, usually floating on their backs with their blond faces to the sky, I thought first of what he had taught me—that sea otters have more hairs per square inch than a medium-sized dog has on its entire body. This density of fur keeps their skin dry even when they dive. It is also what makes their pelts so valuable.

Although they had been hunted to near extinction, first by the Russians and then by Americans, the otter's life seemed a carefree one. They spent their days in the open water or slipping clumsily across the ice. They dove for crabs and urchin and ate their catch while floating on their backs. They played with each other in the surf.

THE DAY I found the dead otter on the beach was a mild one. Continents of clouds moved quickly overhead and wind stroked dark patterns on the surface of the bay. Later, I wouldn't remember exactly why I walked back to the house, drove my station wagon down to the beach with a wheelbarrow in the back, and wheeled the carcass over loose cobbles to bring it home. I knew that taking any part of a sea otter was illegal. But at that moment, there didn't seem to be any way around it. I felt I had to.

The animal was heavy, perhaps sixty pounds, and I used a piece of plywood to lever it onto an old garden table in the yard. The otter stretched about four feet long and its dry fur was a rich brown, like good earth. I turned the carcass over and found no wound or sign of disease. Then, it was like being on automatic pilot. I went into the house and sharpened a small, wood-handled knife against a slate I found at the back of a kitchen drawer. I collected my leather work gloves.

The first cut was hard; the skin resisted the edge of the knife. But when I pushed the tip of the blade into the belly of the otter, it slid in easily. As soon as the carcass was open, I felt terrified and disgusted with myself. But I worked quickly, remembering the cuts I had seen a man make on a dead seal at the local museum. I made shallow slices nearly perpendicular to the skin, detaching dark red muscle that connected the skin to the tissues beneath it. The pelt slowly unpeeled, revealing a sea-green network of tissues that encased the body like woven cloth. A faint smell of rawness dissipated into the winter air. Nothing was stiff like I'd imagined it would be. Yet there was something familiar about the feel of the pelt—its weight and suppleness and the way its edges curled in—though I'd never felt a fresh skin like this before.

I worked all afternoon and when it got dark, I moved into the porch and kept cutting under a yellow light. By then, the burgundy-colored muscle had become blaring red from exposure to the air. It was hard to cut around the legs where a mess of pink fat clutched tightly to the skin. When I got to the first paw, I held it in my hand, and it felt very much like my own. It was worse at the head, which appeared, as animals often do on close look, quite human. The otter's eyes were closed, and small, leathery ears stuck out on the sides of its face. Its jaw was clenched shut, hiding short, sharp teeth, but there was a slight smile on the face. I cut around the head as if slitting the animal's throat and then the pelt was completely free. Exhausted, I covered the animal and fur in plastic, took a shower, and went to bed.

The next day, I drove to the small library in town and found books on preparing hides. I brought home a few small volumes in old-fashioned type written by fur trappers and homesteaders. The hardest work, I learned, was yet to come. Over the next weeks, I would spend hours scraping fat off the skin with the edge of a spoon. I would soak the pelt in salt water multiple times, rinsing and draining, as I had read in one of the books, and then I'd tack it to a piece of plywood and lower it into the crawl space beneath the house where a small heater that kept the pipes from freezing would slowly dry the skin. But that night, as soon as it was dark enough so that no neighbors could see me, I loaded the skinned body back into the wheelbarrow. It was strangely lizardlike now—a bright red body with deep brown head, paws, and tail. The ribs and backbone protruded. I wheeled the carcass down the snowy path and over the cobbles to where the ice ended, freeing gentle waves, and dumped it at the edge of the surf.

In the morning, I walked down the beach to see what had become of the otter. The previous night's high tide had rinsed the bay clean of ice. Already, I missed that blue-white moonscape. Eagles and crows had found the carcass, which had washed down the beach. As I approached, the eagles flew off but the crows stood firm, cawing irritably. When I got close, I saw that the birds had already taken the heart and guts; the otter lay empty.

Weeks later, when the skin dried, the fur was luminous. The longer guard hairs shone silver throughout the brown pelt. When stroked, the fur changed colors like the surface of the sea when wind blows against tide. For a long time, I kept it in a box beneath my bed. The pelt's jagged edge, the nicks, remained a testament to the sense of necessity I had felt, that moment of urgent appropriation. I had taken hold, on my own, of this place.

# 13

# TIDEPOOLS

LUMINOUS RANGE: *n. The maximum distance at which a light can be seen under existing visibility conditions.*

In June, when the tide dropped to its lowest level of the year, kelp fronds collapsed like dull tresses on the shoulders of the rocks. No longer suspended by water, they lay heavily heaped over one another, naked and entwined in the open air. Without water, the under-sea world was suddenly subject to gravity, a force that seemed clumsy and coarse. Falling to the earth was such a mundane thing.

The sound of drying out drenched everything. It was the sound of the sea draining from rocky pools and crevices, the sound of limpets clamping down on rocks, the sound of barnacles closing up shop, like a thousand doors shutting one after another. It always seemed this world was never meant to be exposed. Never meant to feel the weight of sunlight directly upon it, never meant to be slapped open palmed by wind. Such was the exile of low tide. Forgotten for hours by the sea, this margin, this extraordinary edge—it was a coyote's heaven, an oyster-catcher's dream.

When the moon and sun aligned with the Earth at new and full moons, they yanked on the sea in consort, tugging it out of bays and passes, snatching it from coves and shores. These minus tides came twice a month and were printed in the tide books in bright green ink. People scanned the pages for good clamming tides, generally daytime minus tides in the warm months. Green ink also signaled mediocre halibut fishing conditions, as it was harder to keep the bait on the bottom as the shifting tides dragged boats, leaving weights and lines trailing behind.

All week that month there were extremely low tides, while the moon had disappeared from a sliver to nothing. At the beach in town, a vast expanse of deliciously flat sand invited Frisbee and soccer games, gangs of dogs, a man driving golf balls from one end of the beach to the other and back again for hours. A few friends from work and I planned a short camping trip across the bay around the lowest tide at a site that was perfect for exploring rocky tidepools. There were Joel and Marla, the couple building a circular, two-story house in the hills behind town, and Dale and Sharon, who lived fifteen miles out of town. And there was Sue, a biologist who rented a small place not far from town where she lived with a gray cat that a friend had found abandoned in the woods.

We hired a boat that served as a water taxi, stowing our gear in the cabin and under the gunwale to keep it from getting wet, and set off from the harbor for the half-hour ride to the other side of the bay. It was a white sky day, where the movement of clouds overhead was barely perceptible. Common murres zoomed by like bullets. Tufted puffins, with bright orange bills and pale yellow cowlicks of feathers against their black heads, bobbed about and dove out of sight when we approached. We saw sea otters and seals on the way over too, and scanned for the puffs of wet air that signaled whales.

When we landed, the young guy hired for the summer to run the twenty-five-foot boat nosed it up onto the gravel beach and lowered a ladder off the bow into shallow water. I climbed out with two of the others. Those on board passed gear—packed in duffels, backpacks, canvas bags, and dry bags—from the deck to those of us standing in rubber boots in the ankle-deep sea at the bow. Then we unloaded three kayaks and carried them up the beach.

After the boat took off and the sound of its engine faded, we ferried the rest of the gear to the top of the beach. We pitched our tents in spruce needle–strewn depressions between the trees that grew just beyond the border of beach grass and lovage, a tall plant with white, umbrella-shaped flowers and edible leaves that tasted like parsley.

IN THE MONTHS after I left John, I grew more sweet peas than I'd ever imagined, rented four different houses, and forgot about the crab fisherman. I got drunk at bars late into the night, taking over the dance floor with a couple of girlfriends. I'd put on brand-new red lipstick I'd bought from an Anchorage department store makeup counter, where a woman with dark hair slicked back into a perfect ponytail, eyes lined coal-black, and a white lab coat over a streamlined black outfit convinced me she knew exactly what I needed. She pulled out a deep red; I trusted her entirely. Before heading to the bar, I'd grab the sheepskin coat I had found at a used clothing store; the coat was stained and worn, but its wide furry collar made me feel glamorous. On Saturdays, I spent hours thinning carrots or rigging up mini-greenhouses to warm the struggling zucchini plants in my garden. These contraptions of plastic sheeting and wood stakes encouraged the squashes to grow and then rot. I used a borrowed posthole digger to build a fence of spruce posts and gill net to keep moose out of the broccoli, kale, and beets. Most nights, I returned home alone, but occasionally I'd bring home a member of a band touring through from out of town.

That spring, I borrowed a kayak, tied it on the top of my car, and drove up the highway. I camped alone on the far side of a small lake where red-necked grebes were busy building floating nests and savannah sparrows called from the tops of chest-high spruce. In the morning, I hiked to the next lake over, stepping between brown bear tracks freshly laid in the muddy trail. Proud of my initiative to explore, yet terrified of the prospect of bears, as I walked I sang to myself, to the bears, to the kinglets that weren't listening up in the trees. It was a thrill to learn I could heave the boat onto the top of my car and take it down alone. It was a thrill to learn that my own knots held.

Newly alone, necessity required me to adapt, and there were times when I felt like an amputee learning to do those mundane things that had been so easy before. I had to figure out how to get the hundred-pound rototiller I'd rented at the hardware store out of the back of my station wagon. The hardware guys had helped me get it in, but in my driveway, I was on my own trying to get it out. Suddenly simple machines rigged out of scraps of wood were invaluable. Each solution I engineered became a small victory. The diaphanous shower curtain I'd bought used at the Pick 'n' Pay for ten cents billowed to the ceiling once I turned on the water. So I thought of an economical solution: I slid a row of pennies into the bottom seam to weight it down. The coins made a racket as they banged against the inside of the metal tub, but at least my bathroom was dry. I figured out how to conserve heating oil by keeping my small, drafty place freezing cold, and spending a fortune on custom-made, insulated curtains I'd ordered from a catalogue.

There were many things to figure out: how to move a free couch into the house that wouldn't fit through the front door, how to get help from strong men without leading them on; and how to live separately from—but in such close proximity to—a man I had loved and left only a handful of months before. I saw John's car around town more than I saw him. I fought the urge to spend time with him, although a few times, when we did see each other among friends, we orbited around each other awkwardly.

Those months, as I bounced between trying to be the

alluring bar girl, the proficient gardener, the solo explorer, and the resourceful rental house fixer-upper, I felt kaleidoscopic, but not in a dazzling and beautiful way. I felt fragmented into parts, the constant shifts revealed pieces of myself that hadn't been seen—even by me—in a long time. Weekend days opened empty with just my own whims to follow. I wanted most of all to feel independent, but so much autonomy left me dizzy. On the most beautiful days, the sunny and still ones when the perfectly blue sky seemed to be saying there was no reason to be anything but perfectly content, I felt the worst. I wanted someone to whisk me off on an adventure of their devising. No one showed up. So I worked to make headway in the garden. The twenty by twenty–foot patch became my distraction, my refuge. My moods changed like weather, my barometer dependent on so many small things. The garden thrived, but I was lonely. I constantly asked myself: Should I stay?

ON THE SOUTH side of the bay, we were a loose group of friends who seemed to be linked by a penchant for being on the outer side of doors. A few years before, Dale and Sharon had invited John and me to join them on a full-moon skate on a frozen lake where the night was silent except for the groaning of the ice and the scrape of our blades, which wrote a language on the surface of the lake that seemed to be the only thing worth saying. That night cemented a sporadic friendship. Later, we had gone on a too-long spring ski deep in the hills behind town where we crossed and recrossed a river on ice that was dangerously thin. We ran out of snow a half-mile from where we'd parked the car the day before and had to carry our skis the rest of the way, postholing in patches of rotten snow up to our thighs. Along the way, we did not see anyone else, but we saw a dozen moose grouped up along the river, strangely social in a way we'd never known about before. When we finally reached the car, we were exhausted to the point of tears, linked by extreme hunger, crankiness, and eagerness to do it all over again the next spring.

They were all good people, but no one wanted to perch themselves at the bar with me, scanning the room for eyes that were also on the roam. They'd outgrown nights at the bar, they told me. I was a few years too late. I either went alone or stayed home. Loneliness flushed in and out of me.

AFTER PITCHING OUR tents, we took off on our own. Dale and Sharon took the kayaks out; Joel, Marla, and Sue went to scope out a hiking trail up the ridge. I clambered over fallen spruce to a spot at the top of a rocky bluff where the sun fell on a soft patch of yellow-green moss. From here I could see the mouth of the bay, how the inlet on which we camped split into two narrow fjords separated by the green backbone of a mountain ridge, scoured long ago by glacial ice hundreds of feet thick. Three islands anchored themselves near the mouth of this inlet and a rock the shape of an elephant's head reared up out of the water. Although a breeze was raking the water into whitecaps, I was sheltered from the wind. The sun lay across my lap, my chest and face. And so I began to take off my clothes, layer by layer. First the rubber boots and wool socks. Then my fleece coat. Undressing here felt like a supreme luxury; there were so few opportunities in this cold climate to feel the sun on your skin. As I undressed, I heard the emphatic call of a kinglet, and then the spiraling melody of a hermit thrush. Its song turned in on itself and then wound up, higher and higher until it dissipated into the sky. I lay back on the pillowed ground.

Cushioned by moss, I found it easy to forget how thin a skin of green there was between me and the rock which made up the south side of the bay. All of this life—the nuthatches, nagoon berries, devil's club, and thrush—was a simple layer of life above the bedrock. It had accumulated slowly, first with wind and rain turning rock to dust; lichen turning the dust to soil, which provided a bed for things to grow and reproduce on. But now there were columbine and cloudberries, marten and Steller's jays. There were watermelon berries and moose and voles. There was sorrel, and goose-tongue. This whole ecosystem was a fresh cast of the primordial dice. It amounted to a dense but narrow tangle of life above the bedrock and beneath the sky. It was amazing that we had gotten here at all. Maybe it was the sudden burst of vitamin D on patches of my skin that hadn't seen the sun in a long time that made me feel a surge of strength and independence lying there naked by myself. But a short gust of wind set off goose bumps on my skin, reminding me that each feeling was hitched to its opposite, the way centripetal and centrifugal forces keep our universe from collapsing as well as from scattering apart: Strength came with vulnerability, independence with loneliness.

THE NEXT MORNING, we woke up after a night under spruce and sat on the beach with the day, just after 8 A.M., feeling well under way. Marla boiled a pot of water for tea, coffee, and hot oatmeal. She was efficient at the stove—at clearing away cobbles to make a level spot for it on the beach. At priming the pump and lighting it. Water came from a creek down a short trail that led away from our tents and the plywood outhouse a bit farther into the woods. The sky had been peeled of clouds, which had gathered the evening before, and it was already a brilliant blue. I wore all the layers I had brought and sat cross-legged at the top of the beach with both hands clutching a warm mug of tea. I spread cream cheese on a cold grocery store bagel and ate it quickly. The tide was on its way out. I'd checked the tables the night before. Low was a minus 4.7 at 9:58. My watch said 8:11. As the tide retreated and I drank my tea, the dropping bay left a wet edge on shore. There was still over an hour left until the tide sunk to its lowest and as I sat at the top of the gravel beach, rubber boots outstretched before me, the bay continued to drain. When tea and coffee were done, we headed down the beach to where the damp margin was widening. I stepped across rocks studded thickly with barnacles, which crunched beneath my boots, and walked through shards of clamshells strewn between the rocks. Cockles gaped open, revealing a yellowish tongue of flesh inside their deeply grooved shells. They tasted like clams but were chewier; people put them in chowders. Clams shot streams of water from the sandy places between rocks. You could look across the beach and see dozens of them firing off like a timed performance. I wanted to get to the water's edge, where I could see things revealed only at the year's lowest tides. Then I would follow the water back up the beach as the tide changed. Farther down, boulders were embedded in the beach and covered by barnacles and popweed, seaweed with air bladders that looked like pea-sized bubbles within their fronds. There was more than a two-story drop in elevation from the top of the beach to where I squatted at the water's edge. These were two worlds: one tied to land, the other a limb of the sea. Here, I was entering the sea.

Squatting down to my knees to get a closer look, I parted the blades of kelp at the bay's retreating edge to find pools of water beneath the damp fronds. These kelp, exposed only during such extreme low tides, had blades nearly a foot wide. Beneath them, a mass of starfish— some purple, others pink, orange, and red—piled together motionless. A green anemone bloomed between two rocks. I put my finger into its soft center up to the second knuckle. It closed around it, folding in its petal-like arms inside. I tore off a piece of the massive kelp and put it in my mouth. It tasted like al dente lasagna cooked in brine. As we moved about among the kelp and rocks, my friends and I strayed from each other, following our own paths of exploration.

Wet kelp hid crabs of all sizes, which scurried from the light. There were hermit crabs toting snail shells on their backs and a horse crab, which was covered in bristles. I picked it up between my thumb and forefinger, holding it at the back so that its pincers couldn't reach my skin. Its legs paddled uselessly in the air. A purple sea urchin sat on cobbles beneath the kelp. Eventually, when it died, its spines would break off and the animal would rot away, leaving the graceful ringed skeleton you could find bleached white at the top of the beach. Then an oddly shaped crab appeared, with a shell much bigger than its body—an umbrella crab, with wings of shell that stretched beyond its body. I'd never seen a crab like this before—didn't even know these creatures existed. I wanted to share this amazing find with someone. I called over to Sharon, but the sound of my voice was lost into the distance.

A little way up the beach, I lifted a rock to reveal a society beneath. Half a dozen chitons—small, tanklike mollusks with eight-plated shells that clutched tightly to rocks—were clinging to the underside of the rock. There were half a dozen kinds of chitons along this shore; these were in clownish colors: The plates of shell were finely and colorfully striped in pink and white, and the hem of shell around the edge was spotted green, blue, and orange. A sea sponge, which looked like a layer of thick paint, encrusted part of the rock in pink. A delicate star- fish with a body no bigger than a dime and arms as fine as dental floss also clung to the underside of the rock. Another starfish—this one with only four legs and the nub of a fifth growing back—made its home beneath this rock as well.

In the wet puddle beneath where the rock had been, an eel-like gunnel fish the length of my index finger flopped around in its quickly drying world. I picked it up and its slick body flailed against the inside of my closed hand. At the bottom of the palm-sized puddle, pale gray threads radiated from a central point: It was the top of a worm that had built a hard shell in the sand below and extended its tentacles in search of prey. Shrimplike amphipods hopped about in the dampness beneath the rock, and a thimble-sized crab crawled away from the light. Once I had turned over this rock and seen the riot of life beneath it, I wanted to see more. I looked up to see a perfectly clear tidepool just up ahead; I put the rock lid back down on this miniature world and moved on.

I squatted at the edge of a pool as wide as my arms and looked into its surface. Quickly, my reflection dis- appeared, revealing the world in this remnant the sea had left behind. Dozens of hermit crabs sped across the floor of the pool. Another crab appeared in the pool—this one wearing algae along its back, a decorator crab dressed in seaweed for camouflage. Then a black leather chiton with a thick black fleshy rim that felt like wet suede around the edge. These were a favorite subsistence food among Alaska Natives of the region, who called them *bidarki* and ate them boiled. I remembered when John had cut one out of its shell with a pocketknife and we'd eaten it raw while wading in the tidepools. It tasted only of the sea.

I scanned the pool from end to end. Stock-still at one end, where I'd overlooked it before, a tidepool sculpin seemed to hang in the water. This thumb-sized fish had a large mouth and oversized pectoral fins that waved like hands on either side of its head. Small carnivores, they ate barnacles, limpets, copepods, worms, and sometimes each other. My index finger gently broke the surface of the pool and I moved my hand slowly toward it. I wanted to touch the smooth side of this scaleless fish. Members of a large family of small, darting fish, their cousins carried names that conjured stories: saddleback sculpin, buffalo sculpin, fluffy sculpin, staghorn sculpin, and red Irish lord, which had particularly bugged out eyes. I'd been entranced by this small fish when I'd first encountered it on the Oregon coast, amazed first by its ability to blend in perfectly with the colors of its pool. You could move from pool to pool, seeing the same kind of fish, but each would be dressed up in its own uniform. Regardless of whether its backdrop was dominated by pink sponge, green algae, browns, blues, or gray, the sculpin seemed to wear the speckled wallpaper of its home, dissolved into the pool, and disappeared. And this fish returned to its home tidepool, even after high tide washed in and erased the boundaries of its small world. You could take one of these sculpin in a paper cup, I'd heard, and walk them far down the beach. Still, they would find their way home. I remained otherwise motionless as my hand got closer and closer to the fish. At the last moment, it darted under a rock.

I brought my face closer to the pool—the water was thick with minute clear organisms swimming around rapidly. Between them, clear shrimp with red dots surged about. Delicate crimson flowers opened in one corner of the pool: the fancy tops of otherwise plain worms that lived in protective tubes. I could see barnacles waving thready fronds in the water to filter prey. And then something so easily overlooked: a nudibranch, a yellowish sluglike lump no bigger than the end of my thumb with purple spots. This was an unusual find and I was dying to share it, to show everyone—but we'd all wandered off so far from each other it did no good to yell.

As I waded through the tidepools, I wanted to see everything—every anemone, urchin, nudibranch, sculpin, shrimp, amphipod, worm, sea cucumber, crab, sponge, tunicate, periwinkle, and triton. I approached the area like a naturalist, wanting to identify, categorize. I tallied the kinds of starfish I'd seen: true, six-rayed, blood, sunflower, leather, brittle. I tallied the kinds of seaweed: winged kelp, popweed, sugar wrack, black seaweed, and sea lettuce, and their melodic scientific names: alaria, fucus, laminaria, porphyra, ulva.

But names were inadequate to describe these otherworldly creatures. And none of the colors I knew fit
either. Nothing was simply red, blue, yellow, or green.
There were colors I'd never seen before, colors I'd never
even imagined. And everything kept changing: one color
when wet, another when dry. There were stripes and
spots, fringes and threads, borders and plates. The sea's
varied cast formed a complicated play of interlocked life,
each organism adapted perfectly to its role. There were
the cleaners, the eaters, the prey, those that converted the
sun's light to food, those that kept the dead stuff from
cluttering the seafloor.

For a few moments at slack tide, the morning stood
still. The nearly perpetual wind along the bay rested; the
sea didn't move in or out; the blue sky stared; and I kept
my head down, eyes to the pools. But the rest of the world
did go on. Pigeon guillemots let out their high-pitched,
wheezy cries, and a belted kingfisher flew from one
spruce bough to another, calling out in its sharp rattle.
And if I were to come back the next morning, I'd see that
starfish that had been caught far out of the water on this
series of low tides would have migrated down the beach
toward the bay's retreated edge. Their motionlessness
was fiction. As we waded through this ancient terrain,
this naked patch of the sea, the world beat on and on.

I moved up the beach and stopped at the face of a huge
boulder—its seaward size was covered in bright orange
anemones that drooped like hundreds of pairs of breasts.

And over to one side, a rusty-red gumboot chiton had wedged into a gap in the rock. It was the largest of the chitons, and looked like the sole of a boot that had lost its shoe. Beneath the boulder was a wet pocket in the rock where a small pool of water remained. I got on my hands and knees and looked into the darkness. After my eyes adjusted, I could just make out a sloppy mass of red octopus tentacles pocked with white suckers. The octopus shifted when I approached, one tentacle sliding seamlessly against the other, and then was still.

I was a hulking beast next to these delicate beauties. I was an outsider invading places I should never have been at all. To step solely on bare rock was impossible. Eventually, I'd put my boot into a clear pool, mucking up the water. I'd bulldoze a cluster of barnacles with the bottom of my shoe, erasing years of growth. So I pictured myself as six inches tall, clambering gently among nearly head-high boulders the size of grapefruits and wading through seaweed that created slick expanses I could slide across for what would be micro-miles. Were these creatures— sea lemon, whelk, and moon snail—the vestiges of the Big Bang? Were they celestial orphans fallen from space into the edge of the sea? These gelatinous, eyeless, and shelled creatures—were they what we were a million years ago? . . . or perhaps what we would become?

They inhabited the fragments of myself: part armorless sea slug, part well-protected snail. Clawed and spined, and then sometimes boneless, without shells, just a naked piece of flesh. I felt intermittently thrashed and tough, exposed and as if I'd crawled under a very large rock. Then, some nights at the bar, like a fresh piece of detritus thrown by currents to the crabs.

I looked up to see my friends scattered across the acre of exposed rocks. Strong, independent people, I thought. But seeing this colorful and outlandish marine life alone made me intermittently sad.

WHEN THE TIDE started to turn, I saw it in the lowest pools first. Still kelp began to get restless; torn bits of sea-weed started moving up the beach. The pools swelled, and bubbles floated across their surfaces. The bay was coming back to erase what I'd seen over the previous hours. It was taking the pools back, bringing the creatures home. The rising water pushed me back up the beach. But I stopped and looked out across the rocks and the bay. There I was at the edge of the sea. Not a boat person or a carpenter. Not born and raised here, nor even having lived here long. I was no commercial fisherman nor fisherman's wife. The water began sneaking up my boots and would come up fast. I could stand there and pull the bay up around me like a skirt. I could stand there until it pressed against me, holding me tightly, coldly, in-different. But I turned and walked up the beach.

As the bay came back in, it pushed countless jellyfish toward the shore. Some were clear with deep orange cen-ters, while others just gave off a moon white glow. They trailed long ragged tentacles and could have been a fleet of spaceships making their way home. The tidepools filled then disappeared. The rocks were smothered. The seaweed lifted then drowned. It is always quicker leaving than entering another world.

That evening, as clouds hiked up the backs of the mountains toward the summits, on the camp stove I cooked a big pot of mussels I had yanked off nearby rocks. When they opened, they let out juice of the sea which became a rich broth at the bottom of the pot. We shared them all around, picking the bits of meat out of the shells with our fingers and dipping bread into the salty juice.

Joel built a fire on the beach and we sat around it long after dinner, sipping wine out of mugs and passing around a flask of whiskey. There were no stars and there wouldn't be any for weeks. Then, you'd begin to be able to barely make them out with the corner of your eye. If you looked at them straight on, they'd disappear. We watched the sun sink in the north. A gold disc hung in the sky above the sun's exit. It was after 11 P.M., but it was still light enough to read outside. A skiff moved by, breaking the sheet of water that had lain flat after dinner. Small breakers rolled into the beach and broke gently.

People trailed to their tents gradually. The fire faded and the light in the sky gave over a bit of its luster to dark. I brought my toothbrush down to the water's edge where the tide was rising for the second time that day. Brushing my teeth outside had always been one of the joys of an outdoor life. I stepped into the edge of the bay as I brushed. Lights the size of mustard seeds flared up in the water around my boots. I splashed my feet gently, which made the phosphorescence alight like a meteor shower. The sea held stars, moons, and fiery rocks in its midst.

I listened to the sound of the sea card against the cobble beach. I loved that sound of the rocks rolling against each other, wearing each other down into their smooth, round forms. It was a sound, I thought, that could cure almost anything.

I lay down in my tent and listened as the evening chorus of birds simplified. Gradually, melodies were plucked out of the air. First the incessant kinglet broke, then the varied thrush stopped its whistle. I hadn't heard the fox sparrow that had been assembling its complicated song down near the beach for a while. The nuthatch had long since quieted. It was like pulling the instruments out of an orchestra one by one. Finally, it was just a single hermit thrush off in the distance, with its melody sounding sometimes liquid, sometimes metallic, always complete.

# EPILOGUE

This morning I woke up to a silent bay. Windlessness kept the water flat and well-behaved and the pink and blue sky didn't budge. It is fall, and the alder leaves are closing in on themselves. Yards are being picked up, cars winterized. Singles are coupling up for the cold months. Each week, half an hour of light drains away. You can feel the earth's tilt.

In the weeks during which I was finishing this book, the nation's eye was on Alaska like never before. The questions swarmed: What is Alaska all about? Who are Alaskans, really? And what do they stand for?

The answers revealed a knot of contradictions. We represent the country's oil-slicked future; we are anchored in a grimy but abbreviated past; we are the nation's newborn northern heartland; we are exceptional in countless ways—flung far to the north, we are neighbors to foreign territories, and we are good shots and brave in the cold.

Many Alaskans were thrilled just to be put on the map. We weren't that afterthought of a state floating out there in the Pacific, extending a finger to tickle Hawaii's chin. We wanted to be just like everyone else and, at the same time, to be different, better, to be exceptional. We wanted it all.

People who are paying attention say that these desires—for money, oil, gold, and a life away from it all—are threatening Alaska as it has never been threatened before. Our hankerings make us restless—so we move often; our ambitions transform the land and sea. Today, Alaska is warming, melting, and shrinking.

But no natural system is static. The seasons change, the ocean cycles, the earth shakes from time to time, swinging the ceiling lamp like a pendulum over your head. What we don't know is, how quickly will the land and sea outside our windows become unrecognizable? Which of the riches we've come to depend on here—a freezer full of fish, ample berries, nearly endless beds of mussels and clams, silence—will be the first to go?

To live in this place is, in part, to destroy it; that is the paradox—and the responsibility—we live with every day.

I imagine myself in the future, gray-haired, with the backs of my hands like old maps, telling newcomers the same kinds of stories that were told to me when I first moved here. But in my version, the species are different. "We used to head across the bay during minus tides and get as many mussels and clams as we wanted," I might say. "On a lucky dipnetting day, you could catch all the salmon you needed for winter in a single tide." I can't keep that image out of my brain, but I don't want to tell those stories like that. I don't ever want to tell stories about what's *gone*.

What *is* singular about Alaska is that here, we have opportunities that have been lost in most of the rest of the country and much of the world. We have rivers and streams that wind through their natural courses; we have salmon that run up those rivers in their mysterious ways. We have wolves and belugas, walrus and cranes. We have energetic tides, kinetic winds, and the heat of the earth bubbling up within sight. We have water, ice, snow.

Nearly ten years have passed since I moved up to Alaska in the fall just after the cranes left. Since then, I left the state for a time, returned, fell in love, and got married. This year, I missed the cranes' departure—a loss that feels like having to return a library book before you've read the last chapter. But in the next couple of weeks, I hope to catch the swans as they fly by—this year's cygnets as large as their parents but the color of grayed laundry. I watch for them through our living room windows.

A band of clouds is moving down the bay now, and by this afternoon, the tide will switch. I can already see a breeze beginning to rifle through the alders. Constant change is our stasis, the open sea our backyard.

# Acknowledgments

I am indebted countless times over for help and support along my way. I want to first thank my parents, Michael and Susan Weiss. It's because there's always been such a wonderful place to come back to that I've been able to explore.

Thanks to my agent, Kris Dahl, for getting behind this book and to Gillian Blake for her excitement and smart editing.

Thanks to my workshop compatriots at the creative writing program at Columbia University who gutted and filleted my work. Thanks to Richard Locke for his wise editing in the early phases of this project and for helping me see how all of the pieces fit together. I have learned much from other teachers along the way, including Darcy Frey, Lis Harris, Stephen O'Connor, Eva Saulitis, Michael Scammell, Leslie Sharpe, Mark Slouka, and Alan Ziegler.

Two friends I don't ever want to do without—Jessica Stiles and Rose Newnham—provided well-balanced meals of love, feedback, hot mud, and bacchanalia that continue to nourish me.

I can't adequately thank my professor and friend Patty O'Toole—a true Justice of the Peace, Our Lady of Nonfiction, for her cheerleading, friendship, and timely words of wisdom that are always beyond what I feel like I deserve. Sara Marcus has been my most important ally from the time this book began to take shape. A committed reader, she delivered pep talks just when I needed them, and without her big brain, this book would have suffered.

Thanks to Tracy Arensberg, who taught me to see birds, and to Starr Saphir, who hears all the warblers in Central Park. She helped me find the wilderness I needed.

Thanks to my colleagues at the Pratt Museum, a small museum with big ideas about the deep connections between people and place.

And I owe thanks to many people who shared their knowledge and experiences, including: Ed Berg, Joel Cooper, Holly Cusack-McVeigh, Tom Doolittle, Lois Epstein, Dave Erikson, Carmen Field, Steve Fishback, Jeff Fox, Steve Gibson, Brian Hirsch, Janet Klein, Ray Kranich, Sue Mauger, Ken Maynard, Thomas McDonough, Dennis McMillan, Ken Moore, Chris Oldham, Rob Rosenfeld, Mara Schwartz, Doug Schwiesow, Rick Sinnott, Larry Smith, Tom Smith, Michele Stenger, Charlie Trowbridge, Betsy Webb, and Steve Zimmerman. Errors are my own.

Deep thanks to the waters and landscapes that have inspired my writing and to the people who work hard to create and maintain beauty in the world around us, as well as birds, fish, predators, clean water, and wilderness. Some of the entities they work through are Cook Inletkeeper, Alaska Marine Conservation Council, Kachemak Heritage Land Trust, Kachemak Bay Conservation Society, and Center for Alaskan Coastal Studies.

Finally, thanks to my husband, Bob Shavelson, for his love, generosity, and potent backrubs. We're at the beginning; I'm excited for more.